Mostly Mittens

Charlene Schurch

Mostly Mittens

Traditional Knitting Patterns from Russia's Komi People

Charlene Schurch

Lark Books

Dedication

*To Fred, who encouraged, listened, and most of all helped
create a life where there is space for my knitting.*

Editor: Jane LaFerla
Art Directors/Production: Elaine Thompson, Chris Bryant
Photographer: Evan Bracken
Art Production: Hannes Charen
Illustrator: Orrin Lundgren
Proofreader: Val Anderson

Library of Congress Cataloging-in-Publication Data
Schurch, Charlene.
    Mostly mittens : traditional knitting patterns from Russia's Komi people /
Charlene Schurch. -- 1st ed.
        p.   cm.
    Includes index.
    ISBN 1-57990-059-3
    1. Knitting--Russia (Federation)--Komi--Patterns.   2. Mittens--
Russia (Federation)--Komi.   I. Title.
TT819.R92K657   1998
746.43'20432-dc21   98-4632
                                                 CIP

10 9 8 7 6 5 4 3 2 1

First Edition

Published by Lark Books
50 College St.
Asheville, NC 28801, US

Copyright © 1998, Charlene Schurch

Distributed by Random House, Inc., in the United States,
        Canada, the United Kingdom, Europe, and Asia
Distributed in Australia by Capricorn Link (Australia) Pty Ltd., P.O. Box 6651,
        Baulkham Hills Business Centre, NSW 2153, Australia
Distributed in New Zealand by Tandem Press Ltd., 2 Rugby Rd.,
        Birkenhead, Auckland, New Zealand

Printed in Hong Kong by Oceanic Graphic Printing Productions, Ltd.

All rights reserved

ISBN 1-57990-059-3

Contents

Introduction

In presenting the patterns of the Komi people, I have tried to preserve a small portion of the world's knitting traditions that otherwise might be lost. As you knit these logical and sophisticated patterns, consider that they have been passed down through the generations in an oral rather than a written tradition. In working through the projects, I hope you will gain more than a few new patterns. I hope that you will experience the thrill of exploring older knitting traditions, and by placing them in a modern context, that they will speak to you from the past, as they did to me, through the language of our stitches.

—Charlene

The Search

Reading Richard Rutt's *A History of Hand Knitting* made a deep impression on me. Previously I hadn't really given much thought to knitting traditions other than considering the beautiful, perennially fashionable Scandinavian sweaters. Now I found knitting could be of academic interest as well. Since I love to knit, the thought that I could research, share, and thus preserve traditions for other knitters to enjoy appealed to me; it was a way that I could touch the past and affect the future. I was captivated by the idea and became inspired to do my own research. But where to begin?

Being of Czech heritage, I searched Rutt's index and reviewed the book for related references. During this investigation, I found there was a gap in the literature of the knitting of the Slavic people; Czechs, Poles, Bulgarians, Yugoslavians, and the Soviet Union (save for the lace shawls). I knew these people had to knit because of Eastern Europe's severe winters–my search was on.

Discovering the Komi

At the New York Public Library, I found two intriguing little volumes by the same author, Galina Nikolaevna Klimova, about the textile traditions of the Komi, whose homeland is in northeast European Russia, just west of the Ural Mountains and close to the Arctic Circle. *Uzornoe Viazanie Komi* is a study of Komi knitting, and *Komi Textile Ornamentation*, published later, looks at the development of Komi textile ornamentation from a genealogical point of view as it is applied to Komi knitting, weaving, and embroidery. The pictures of the mittens and stockings were very different from what I had seen before but were reminiscent of some of those found in Lizabeth Upitis' book of Latvian mittens. It wasn't Czech, but at that point, at least, I thought it was Slavic. As I later learned, the Komi are related to the Finns and Estonians.

I found the pictures compelling enough to have Klimova's texts translated. I was fortunate enough to have a native Siberian (Buryiat) and member of the Russian department at Wesleyan University help me. In addition to the translations, he was able to place the Komi in a cultural and human context that caught my imagination. I wanted to know more and was off to any library I could find for background information. Since the Komi are a Russian ethnic minority and didn't figure in any of the major political events of Russian history, the card catalogue yielded precious little.

What I did learn about the Komi of today was the age-old story of assimilation and change that has affected similar groups of native people around the world. At the turn of the twentieth century native Russians began migrating north. Shortly thereafter, the homeland of the Komi was found to have rich reserves of oil and natural gas. This discovery brought an even greater influx of workers, who gradually overshadowed the older Komi culture and traditions with their own. Faced with this information, I realized how vital it was to help preserve what I could.

The Komi People

The Komi people are of the Finno-Ugric language group. This group is small today, with roughly 22.5 million people speaking one of its languages; the Hungarians, with 14 million people, are the largest representation, followed by the Finns at 5 million, and the Estonians at 1 million. All of the Finno-Ugric people were originally from Central Asia in the Ob River Basin, and migrated at various times from before 400 A.D. to sometime in the Middle Ages.

The Komi were in Russia by 1000 to 1200 A.D. Originally a migratory, reindeer-herding people, they began establishing a livelihood dependent on farming, fishing, and hunting reindeer around 1700. As late as the mid-1950s, the Komi were still living in village-type communities. Today there are

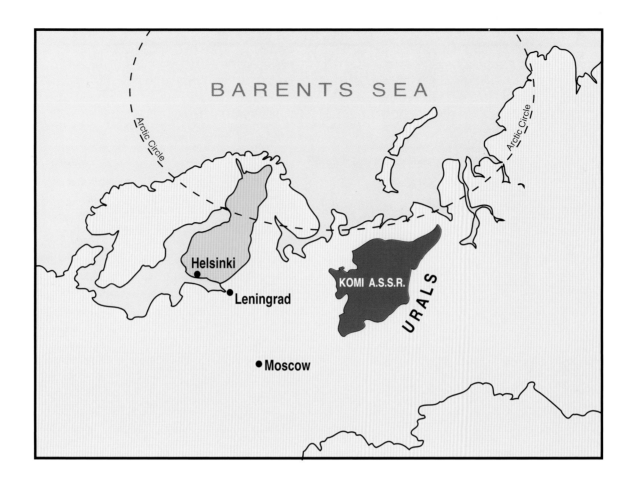

only about 285,000 Komi speakers. Russia considers them one of the 26 recognized ethnic minorities and they form an independent republic.

Komi Dress

The Komi, like many ethnic groups, began to abandon their traditional dress in favor of other styles as they became assimilated into a larger culture. Before that time, women were responsible for making all the clothing for their families. They had to rely on their crops and animals to provide the raw materials for their garments. Traditionally, the Komi would wear a tunic made from reindeer skin. In the winter, linen undershirts were worn under the reindeer skin. A visitor to the area in the seventeenth century noted that the men and women dressed alike; even the patterns on the mittens and stockings were identical.

Women would spin flax, hemp, and wool from plants and animals that they raised themselves. The men were responsible for carving the spindles out of wood. Vegetable and mineral dyes were used until the mid-nineteenth century when chemical dyes became available. The needles for knitting were originally made of wood or bone. When steel needles became available, the Komi would purchase or trade them for goods.

Before they could marry, girls had to weave at least two dozen towels, 10 yards of cloth, make three dozen pairs of stockings, the same amount of mittens, and one or two dozen shirts. The quantity and quality of work became the bride's recommendation. In order to fill this order, girls began preparing for their wedding at the age of 10. All the goods were then presented to the family and relatives of the bridegroom at the wedding.

Komi Knitting

With a basic understanding of the traditional Komi culture and lifestyle, I was able to turn to Klimova's books. Her text deals mostly with patterns rather than the specific construction techniques. What she does offer about construction is based on simple observation: the stockings are knit with patterning on the leg with the feet knit in one color; the same patterns are used for both men and women; mittens and stockings with more complex patterns are originally made for festive occasions, then as they age they're worn for everyday.

Klimova notes that the simpler patterns were knit by women who could not handle the more complicated ones–just as today, some people are more capable than others. It was refreshing to read and consider that not every nineteenth century knitter was doing museum quality work.

The fundamental design element of the Komi patterns is the diamond. Klimova takes the search for the genesis of this back to the second century B.C. Pottery pieces from that period, with diagonal patterns, have been found in areas of what is today Kazakstan, the Southern Urals, and Southern Siberia. These locations are within the original home of the Finno-Ugric People. Scholars believe these diamond-based patterns were first used on "soft" materials such as in weaving and embroidery, before they were used for decorating ceramics.

The Komi Influence

As with any research, unanticipated connections often surface. Without seeking it out, I found an interesting link that shows how knitting traditions pass from one culture to another, and how they can influence and affect generations of knitters around the world.

Eve Harlow, in *The Art of Knitting*, reports that two-color knitting fragments from the sixteenth century were found in Latvia, the Komi Republic, the Karelian district of Russia, Estonia, and the Caucasus. Alice Starmore, in her *Book of Fair Isle Knitting*, traces the importation of colored knit pieces from Estonia or Finland, and asserts this was the event that began the beautiful Fair Isle tradition in Scotland.

The languages spoken by the people living in the areas mentioned by both Harlow and Starmore are Finno-Ugric. In researching Komi traditions, I have found that all of the Finno-Ugric textile work share a similarity of ornamentation; photographs of their textile work show the complex diagonal geometric pattern is clearly part of their culture. Now as I look at the sophisticated Fair Isle pieces, I can clearly see the influence of the older Finno-Ugric traditions. For me, it was one more example of how the common language of our stitches extends beyond the boundaries of time, cultural differences, and geography.

Komi men wearing patterned knit socks.

From Kalishnikova,
National Costumes of The Soviet People, 88.

Komi Patterns

The story of the pattern knitting of the Komi is unique as well as universal. The Komi as preliterate people held their patterns in memory. Therefore, most of the patterns that evolved did so around a system that made remembering them easier. Every Komi village had their own distinct variations of the basic patterning, and a person who knew the patterns could tell where another person was from by looking at their knitted garments.

All of the Komi knitted goods of the late nineteenth and early twentieth century were knit with at least two colors. Stripes were used on the cuffs of mittens and on the legs of stockings, providing a logical and easy way to introduce multiple colors—perfect for beginning knitters.

While knitting the design with two strands (or more) of colored yarn was a more complicated process, it created a beautifully patterned piece and a warmer garment. Unlike knitting with a single color, the yarn that's not being knit is carried along the back creating "floats," which make an extra layer that traps warm air. For the Komi, any additional

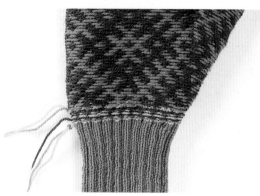

By turning a mitten inside out, you can see the floats that create an extra layer for warmth.

warmth must have been a welcome necessity during their long and brutal winters.

Combining Patterns

The appeal of Komi patterning is its simple symmetry. By using stripes of color, borders of pattern, and allover designs (called reticulations) of complex diagonal geometric patterning, the Komi developed a palette of pattern choices. By combining them in attractive and imaginative ways, they created their beautiful knit stockings and mittens. Add the dimension of color, and the possibilities seem almost endless.

The Komi Basic Patterns are repeats—four stitches wide and four rounds high—which use repeating pattern stitches to build the design. At first glance, patterns constructed this way may look complicated. As you look closer, you'll begin see how a few stitches, stacked line upon line, create a clever pattern that's easy to knit.

Most of the borders and reticulations that the Komi use are created upon a system where all the lines of the pattern are three stitches wide, and the pattern of the foreground and background are balanced (e.g., as much black as white). The patterns can range in complexity from repeats of 6 to 72 stitches. These patterns are profound in their creation since they look more complicated than they are, yet are simple to hold in memory.

Reticulations are created with the principle of a background cross made of five stitches (three wide and three high). This results in every third row being worked as three dark and three light stitches, known as three by three (3 dark x 3 light) patterns. The other rows are worked in one, three, or five stitches before changing color. These are easy to knit and make a nice tight fabric with relatively short floats on the back. (See the following chart.)

The diagonal-shaped pattern is aligned on the vertical and horizontal axis. Sometimes a portion of an allover design is selected for use as a border. A favorite pattern is a seven-row or septenary border. These are similar in construction to the reticulation but only have one axis.

Over time there seems to have been some editing of the patterns. There are a few septenary borders that have some vertical lines, rather than being created like the reticulations. In addition, some wide borders and reticulations have had their pattern lines extended to five or seven stitches wide. While still maintaining the diagonal geometric of the original pattern, they look more airy than the denser, traditional patterns.

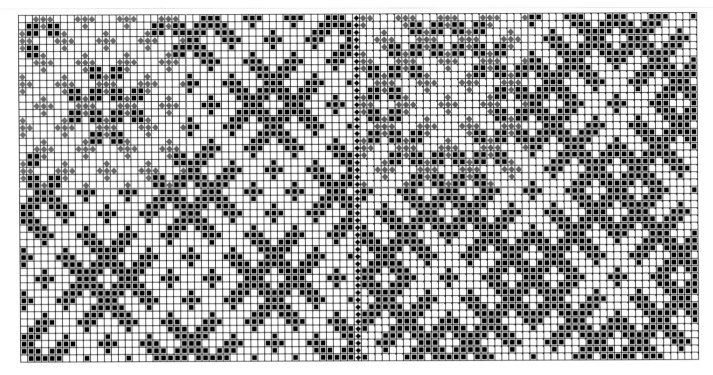

As you can see the patterns are created from a grid of crosses.

The star or snowflake pattern, very popular among the knitters of northern Europe, was introduced to the Komi from Russian migration in the late nineteenth century (see Mitten 31, page 90). The one used in Komi knitting is similar to the one used in Norway, yet the Komi pattern retains its own variations.

As you look at the patterns and work with them, you'll begin to see their possibilities. The amount of the pattern you use affects the final design. Many of the septenary border patterns are taken from larger reticulations and wide borders, while wide borders can be expanded to create reticulations.

Working with the Projects

This book contains charts and instructions for 36 mittens. Since the Komi also knit patterned socks, I included instructions for two socks, one with a shaped heel, one with a peasant heel, to show how the patterns can work on them. I've also included two cap instructions in case you might want a matching cap for your mittens. The instructions for the socks and caps follow the mitten projects.

I've arranged the mitten projects in chapters according to their pattern system. Each chapter progresses from the easiest to the most complex. At the beginning of each chapter, you'll find detailed explanations of the pattern system with the mitten projects following. If you're a novice knitter, you may want to

start with one of the projects from the Basic Patterns until you feel comfortable enough to work the more complex ones. Fundamentally, the only difference in knitting the Basic Patterns and the more complex ones is attention to detail.

Just as a picture is worth a thousand words, sometimes the best way to decipher patterns is to work a few quick samples. Once you begin to translate the words into stitches, your hands will take over, helping you understand where words often fail. As you knit, you'll begin to experience the beauty and logic of the Komi system as you watch the pattern unfold.

Positioning the Patterns for Designing Mittens, Socks, and Caps

With their strong geometric lines, balanced light and dark coloration, and large repeats, Komi patterns require some thought about positioning them on small items. Graph paper or a good charting program on the computer is a great help, if not a necessity.

There are two basic rules for positioning the patterns:

1) Center the pattern. Match the focal point of the pattern with the focal point of the garment. Be aware that since you are centering the design, you will need to start knitting somewhere other than at the beginning of the pattern such as at a side seam.

2) Since Komi patterns all have an even number of stitches, place them on a visual ground with an odd number, so the central stitch is in the middle and the edges are the same. Not only is this more attractive, you'll find it's much easier to keep track of your pattern as you knit in the round.

In positioning a pattern for a mitten, start by creating a full chart of the whole hand. Center the pattern on the hand so the pattern at the tip ends either in a complete repeat or at an attractive point in the pattern. *Note:* Always begin at the tip since a partial pattern at the cuff is easier to overlook then an incomplete pattern at the tip. Then, fill in the pattern for the rest of the mitten. The chart below is taken from Mitten 15. It illustrates pattern placement for creating an effective design.

There are several ways to position the design on the thumb. You can use a separate pattern altogether, as for Mitten 27. Or, you can copy the center of the mitten pattern onto the thumb chart. To do this, first take a look at the pattern and decide if you like it. You may want to move the pattern over by half a pattern, as for Mitten 31, so the whole star is on the thumb instead of half the star on each side with a center design.

In positioning the pattern for a sock with a cuff, place the pattern so it will start or end at the cuff in a logical and attractive spot. If you want the whole sock to be patterned, place the pattern at the tip of the toe first, as you would at a mitten tip, then fill in the pattern for the rest of the sock.

Caps present a fun opportunity for use of color and pattern. However, the shaping of a cap can be a bit of a problem when considering where to position the pattern. An easy way is to use one of the border patterns, placing it at the cuff. Then, use a smaller pattern or a series of narrow borders as you work toward the top of the cap.

Using the Patterns for Designing a Sweater

Although I haven't included sweater instructions in this book, more experienced knitters may want to expand some of the patterns to make larger garments. As you begin creating your design, follow the two rules for positioning a pattern on an item as you would for a mitten. Remember that the focal points for a sweater will be the shoulders. Make sure that you center your pattern, both front and back, so it will be complete or will end in a logical place. This means that you need to calculate an accurate gauge swatch to know how many rows you'll have between ribbing and shoulder, then adjust accordingly.

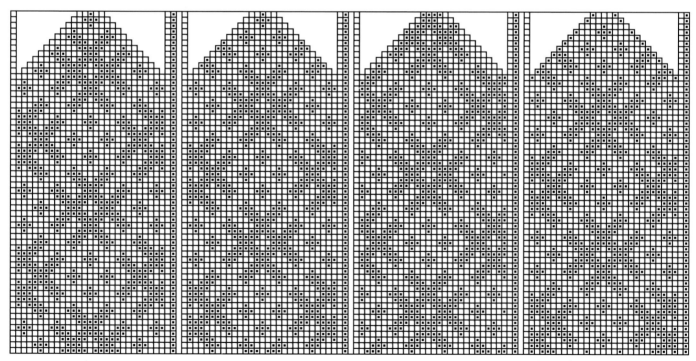

1) Design for Mitten 15.   2) Works well, but not as strong as 1.   3) Pattern is off-center.   4) Weak lines at top.

Since these are large patterns, you can use the device of seam stitches, like those created for the mittens and socks (see page 16), or a vertical septenary border to provide a visual break when dividing the front and back. For further reference, Alice Starmore offers a detailed discussion of designing patterned sweaters in her *Book of Fair Isle Knitting* and her *Charts for Colour Knitting*.

In Praise of Mittens

TEN REASONS FOR MAKING MITTENS
YOUR NEXT PROJECT

1) Mittens are knitting in its highest form; you create the fabric and shape it at the same time.

2) They're small—materials aren't costly.

3) They're extremely portable—you can work on them anywhere.

4) You can complete a project quickly.

5) Though small, they are a most generous gift.

6) You can try new patterns and colors, gaining confidence before tackling a much larger project.

7) They're an opportunity to display your talent all winter long.

8) When you give hand-knit mittens to family and friends, you're also showing them your concern for their comfort in a beautiful way.

9) They're fun to wear, whether you're making a snowman, shoveling snow, or walking the dog.

10) You can wear the same pair of mittens everyday, and unlike a shirt, no one will ever accuse you of not changing your clothes.

Basic Techniques

Yarn

The needle size and gauge on yarn labels are typically for a sweater or garment that needs some drape to the fabric. For mittens, caps, and socks, I prefer to knit a much denser fabric. This has several advantages: it is more windproof; it will wear longer; and, depending on the yarn, will shrink less. Knitting the mittens in fine yarn at a tight gauge shows the lovely Komi patterns to their best advantage, since knitting with bulky yarn and large needles would only show a small portion of the pattern. I've also found that working with two or more colors knit at many stitches to the inch creates a wonderfully rich-looking fabric.

The yarns used in this book are labeled Sport and Fingering weight, and are all 100% wool (except for one pair of socks). It is my strong opinion that wool is the superior choice for mittens since it offers better insulation than manmade yarns. If you like to wash mittens often, or are knitting mittens as a gift for someone who likes to wash everything in the washing machine, I suggest you substitute sock or super-wash wool yarns.

The mitten instructions are "as knit," giving specific yarn and needle sizes. If these yarns are not available to you, there are many other wonderful yarns that you can successfully substitute. Keep in mind when substituting yarns that you must keep the same approximate weight-to-length ratio (grams/ounces to yards, or grams to meters). For best results, read your labels, compare the ratios, and substitute as closely as possible.

Needles

Double-pointed needles are a necessity for knitting a seamless pair of mittens. I use the 7-inch (18-cm) needles. If you aren't afraid of losing your stitches, you may want to try the finger-sized, 4-inch (10-cm) needles. They're big enough for knitting a child's mitten and are somewhat easier to manage.

Some knitters prefer using the 11-inch (28-cm) circular needles for socks and mittens. This is a matter of choice. I'm uncomfortable using circular needles since the mittens I've knit are too small around for that style of needle. However, I've included instructions for knitting with circular needles on page 108.

You may need to give your hands time to adjust to using double-pointed needles, particularly in a smaller needle size. Just be patient. I find that aluminum or wooden needles are more gentle on the hands and lighter when knitting a very tight gauge. Be careful when using the smaller sizes of wooden needles; they may break if you hold them too tightly. Always look for double-pointed needles with sharp points rather than rounded points, since this makes decreasing easier.

The instructions for the mittens are written for five needles (four holding the work and one to knit). By distributing the stitches evenly, the front and back are kept separate, and it is easier to know exactly where you are in the chart and on the mitten. You will always start knitting at either the beginning or the middle of the chart.

Gauge Swatches

When working in the round, you must knit the gauge swatch in the round. Many knitters (me included) have a different gauge with the same yarn and needle size when knitting in the round than when knitting flat. A good gauge swatch is 4 x 4 inches (10 x 10 cm). You can knit 4 inches (10 cm), take it off the needles, then cut to measure it flat. Or, you can knit 8 inches (20.5 cm) around and lay it flat to measure. I find I get a more accurate gauge measurement by counting whole stitches and dividing by inches (cm) in fractions.

Making gauge adjustments before beginning a project will save you problems later on. You may need to adjust your needle size if your swatch doesn't match the gauge. If the swatch is larger than the gauge, try using a smaller needle size; if the swatch is smaller, try larger needles. You may think a half-stitch variance in gauge, either plus or minus, won't make much of a difference in the finished item. However, it can create a mitten that is either larger and longer, or smaller and shorter than you want.

Sizing

The mitten projects are either in child or adult sizes medium and large, with the child's size large equivalent to an adult's size small. Since mittens need to fit the hand comfortably with a little room to spare, take accurate measurements for a correct fit. Measure around the knuckles, then add an inch (2.5 cm) to provide extra room for the hand and the floats on the inside. Remember–it's the trapped air that makes a mitten warm. If you're undecided as to which size to knit, you'll be more satisfied choosing the larger one. As you can see from the chart, hand circumference and length are the same in classic mitten sizing.

Size	Circumference	Height
Child's medium	6 in. (15 cm)	6 in. (15 cm)
Child's large	7 in. (18 cm)	7 in. (18 cm)
Adult medium	8 in. (20.5 cm)	8 in. (20.5 cm)
Adult large	9 in. (23 cm)	9 in. (23 cm)

Knitting With Two Colors

It is my opinion that right-handed or left-handed knitting should be added to the list of topics, such as religion and politics, that can't be argued successfully. It seems that every knitter will defend the method with which they're most familiar. Whether right- or left-handed, there are three ways to hold the yarn while knitting with two colors: both colors in the left hand, both colors in the right hand, or one color in each hand (see Figure 1). As part of full disclosure,

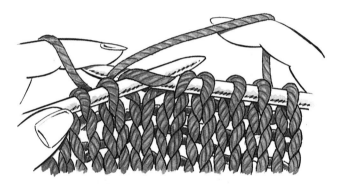

Figure 1

I should state that when knitting with one color I knit with the yarn in my left hand.

Note that whichever method you use, be consistent throughout the knitting of a pair of mittens. The yarn that's held above the other will be the one to stand out in the pattern. Decide which will be which in the beginning, so the pattern will read the same throughout the mitten.

Casting On and Beginning to Knit

I prefer the long-tail cast on since it produces a firm yet elastic edge. It's best to cast on over two double-pointed needles to prevent the cast-on edge from being too tight. (If you can adjust the tension, cast on using one needle.) Make a slip knot at a distance from the end of the yarn approximately four times the length needed for the stitches you'll cast on.

Hold the needles in your right hand with the tail hanging forward and the ball end behind. Insert your left thumb and index finger between the two strands, spread them apart, and grab the strands with the last three fingers of your left hand, spreading them apart slightly. Think of the loop on the thumb as a stitch on the left-hand needle and the yarn

around the index finger as the yarn on a continental knitter's left finger when knitting.

Bring the needles under the front strand of the thumb loop, then up and over the front strand of the index-finger loop. Catch the yarn, bringing it under the front of the thumb loop, using it to adjust tension on the new stitch (see Figure 2).

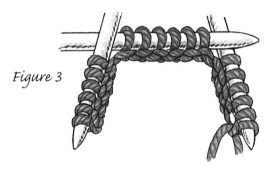

Figure 2

Distribute the stitches onto either three or four double-pointed needles, then join them. Be careful not to twist the stitches, making sure that the cast-on edge lies below the needles all the way around (see Figure 3).

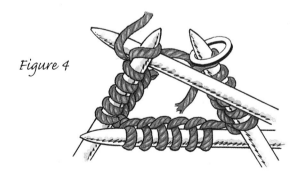

Figure 3

When working the ribbing, you want to begin each needle with a knit stitch. Pick up the empty needle with your right hand and begin to knit. After knitting the first stitch, draw the running thread tightly to close the circle (see Figure 4).

Figure 4

When you have finished knitting the stitches on the first needle, transfer the empty needle from left to right hand and begin working on the second needle. I find the placement of the needles as shown in Figure 4, to be comfortable while knitting by preventing the other needles from getting in the way. Remember to keep the tension of the running thread between stitches the same as at the junction of two needles; this will prevent a "ladder" effect of loose stitches.

Cuff

There are several cuff designs that are attractive and work well with the mitten designs in this book; plain ribbing, corrugated ribbing, and patterned two-color knitting. Plain ribbing (k2, p2) is my favorite, and the simplest. It's highly elastic and grabs the wrist snugly.

Corrugated ribbing, where the knit stitches and purl stitches are in different colors, is more decorative and colorful than plain ribbing, but less elastic than single-color ribbing. You can introduce other colors by changing the colors of the knit or purl stitches. Follow these instructions for corrugated ribbing. Round 1: ★ k2 MC, k2 CC ★ repeat around. (Knitting all stitches on the first round avoids the purl bump). Round 2: ★ k2 MC, p2 CC ★ repeat around. While working this ribbing, be sure to keep both working yarns in back of the work.

Patterned cuffs in this book use the Komi patterns. The cast on is the Scandinavian twisted edge with two colors. The length of the patterning is about the same length as a ribbed cuff with an added ¾-inch (2-cm) band of single-color ribbing between the cuff and the mitten body, providing a snugger fit that keeps the wrist warmer.

The following instructions are for the **Scandinavian twisted edge**. Begin with the long-tail cast on over one needle using two colors, holding one color over the thumb and the other over the index finger. Make two slip knots; do not count them as stitches, slipping them off before you begin to knit. Round 1: ★ k1 MC, k1 CC ★ repeat around. Round 2: Bringing both colors to the front of the work, ★ p1 MC, p1 CC ★ repeat around. After each stitch is worked, place the yarn to the left, bring the other on top and work. Round 3: ★ p1 MC, p1 CC ★ repeat around. After each stitch is worked, place the yarn to the right, bring the other yarn from the bottom and work.

After working Round 2, the yarns will be twisted and difficult to work. The twist created in Round 3 is in the opposite direction and will untwist the yarns from Round 2, making you ready to work the pattern.

Increasing

An attractive thumb gore needs an increase that is unobtrusive and with a mirror image. There are two types that provide this feature, the Make 1 (M1) and Make 1 Reverse (M1R), and the strand increase (inc).

To make the M1 and M1R begin with a backward loop over the needle, knit one and make a loop in the reverse way over the needle, as shown in Figure 5. Place a marker. As you

Figure 5

work in the round after the M1, work the first increase stitch in the standard manner, then knit the second increase stitch (M1) through the back of the loop to tighten the stitch and make it flatter.

To make the strand increase for the right sides, insert the left needle from back to front into the horizontal strand between the last stitch worked and the next stitch on the left needle. Knit this strand through the front of the loop to twist the stitch.

To make the strand increase for the left side, insert the left needle from the front to back into the horizontal strand between the last stitch worked and the first stitch on the left needle. Knit this strand through the back of the loop to twist it. This method of increasing looks similar to the M1 and M1R.

Tools

In addition to yarn and needles you will need a tapestry needle, a pair of scissors, and a crochet hook to pick up the three stitches that complete the thumb. I've also found using a magnetic board with a magnetic ruler to be very helpful. I put the chart on the board, placing the ruler just above the row I'm working. This lets me see what I've completed and where I am without the temptation to inadvertently knit ahead. These boards are available at knitting and craft stores.

Mitten Instructions

Since the Komi used their patterns on mittens and stockings, they were knit in the round as multiples of the total number of stitches in the knitted article. For example, a mitten knit with 72 stitches around could have a 36-stitch pattern repeat. However, using this repeat limits you to 36, 72, 108 or 144 stitches. I've found it's very hard to get two sizes of adult mittens in that range. In designing the mittens it was often necessary to use partial repeats.

To work with this, I used three stitches as "seam" stitches in a contrast color (CC), main color (MC), and contrast color (CC). These can also be called delimiter stitches, since they create a boundary between the patterns on the front and palm. Without this device, it would be difficult to create multiple sizes while showing the patterning to its best advantage.

The seam stitches serve several other purposes. They anchor both working colors to prevent a float that is too long, as would happen if the patterns were just cut off at the seam. They also help maintain the proper length of floats for decreasing at the tip. And the stitches help you avoid the "jog" you get when knitting patterns in the round, giving the eye a resting place so the match is not visually jarring.

I've made the mittens with a gored thumb. This seems to work perfectly with the seam stitches, which not only provide boundaries for the gore but add a handsome design element. I've also incorporated seam stitches in both sock patterns and the cap on page 103.

How to Use the Charts

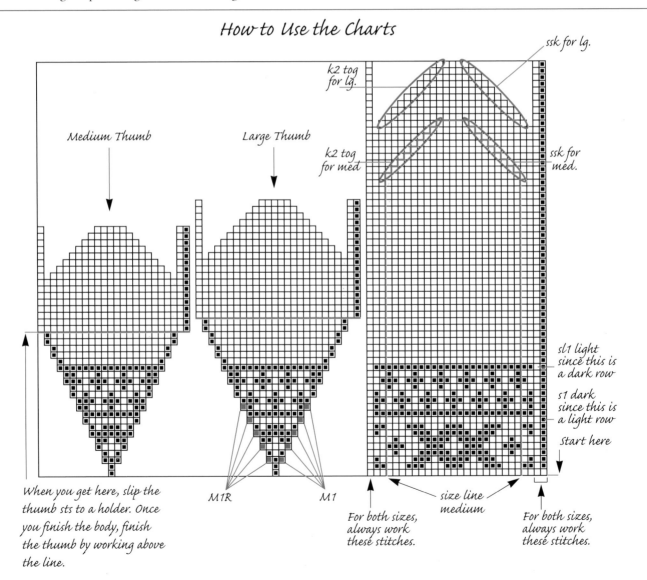

ssk for lg.

k2 tog for lg.

Medium Thumb

Large Thumb

k2 tog for med

ssk for med.

sl1 light since this is a dark row

s1 dark since this is a light row

Start here

When you get here, slip the thumb sts to a holder. Once you finish the body, finish the thumb by working above the line.

M1R

M1

size line medium

For both sizes, always work these stitches.

For both sizes, always work these stitches.

The thumb gore grows from the center seam stitch on the left of the chart. The boundary stitches create an attractive design. Once you get to the "crotch" of the thumb, slip the stitches on a holder, then complete the body.

Since the charts show two sizes, begin by selecting the size you need. Note the side seam stitches running along the sides of the chart; whatever size you choose, remember to include the side seam stitches as you knit. Also note there are two complete thumb charts for each size.

Even though these mittens can be worn on either the right or left hand, assume that you are knitting for the right - meaning you should begin reading the chart on the bottom right. You'll be knitting in the round, and will knit the back of the mitten first, then the thumb stitches, then the palm. When you get to the "crotch" of the thumb gore (corresponding to where the thumb attaches to the hand), you will place the thumb stitches on a holder and finish knitting the body of the mitten. When the body is complete, you will finish working the thumb.

The first stitch on the chart is called the center seam stitch, followed by the second seam stitch. Next come the pattern stitches. Note how the thumb gore grows out of the center seam stitch on the left side of the chart. As you work the thumb stitches to the crotch, omit the center seam stitch for the palm of the mitten (the second time you work around the chart). Once you complete the thumb gore to the crotch of the thumb and place the stitches on the holder, you will resume knitting the center seam stitch as you complete the body of the mitten.

Instructions

Individual information for the mittens will give you the yarn, gauge, and needles to use. You will also have the cuff style and length, as well as the size of the reticulation repeat (if applicable). The following example explains the basic procedure for a child's size medium and large; an adult's size medium and

large in 8 sts = 1 inch (2.5 cm); and adult's size medium and large in 10 sts = 1 inch (2.5 cm). The given numbers correspond to this sequence.

Cast On: 48 (56); 64 (72); 80 (92) sts. Work cuff (see page 15) for 3¾" (9.5 cm); 3½" (9 cm); 3¾" (9 cm). If you have been knitting the cuff on three needles, rearrange the stitches on four needles for knitting the body; it's easier to keep your place on the chart when the stitches are divided this way.

Work the body of the mitten in two-colored knitting in stockinette stitch. (When knitting in the round, stockinette stitch is made with all knit rounds, no purl.) On the third round, after you've knit the first 24 (28); 32 (36); 40 (46) stitches, start the thumb increase on the third needle with M1, k1, M1R. Remember, the thumb chart replaces the center seam line at the left side of the mitten chart. When knitting the palm, skip the center seam stitch and knit from the thumb chart instead.

For now, all the thumb stitches are on the third needle. When you have 11 thumb stitches, transfer 5 of them to the second needle, placing a marker between the hand and thumb stitches. Leave the remaining 6 on the third needle. From now on, the middle stitch of the thumb gore will be the first stitch on the third needle.

When the thumb gore is completed, there should be 21 (23); 25 (27); 31 (35) stitches for the thumb, including the seam stitches. Work the next round even. When you reach the thumb on the next round, use a tapestry needle to slip the thumb stitches to a thread. Cast on one MC stitch to replace the one seam stitch taken up by the thumb gore. Knit across the palm side of the mitten. There will now be a total of 48 (56); 64 (72); 80 (92) stitches, with 13 (14); 16 (18); 20 (23) stitches on each of 4 needles.

Follow the chart, once for the back and once for the palm, until you are ready to decrease for the tip as shown on the chart. Keep the seam stitches in the pattern when decreasing. *When you are knitting a single-color round, slip the alternate color seam stitch from the round below to maintain seam line integrity.*

To decrease, begin with the first needle and k2 from the chart (one MC, one CC). SSK in pattern color, knit to the end of the needle. On the second needle, knit to within 3 stitches of the end of the second needle, k2tog in pattern, k1 (CC). On the third needle, repeat as for the first needle. On the fourth, repeat as for the second needle.

Continue to decrease this way for every round, until 16 stitches remain, 4 sts on each needle (5 pattern stitches plus 3 seam stitches for both the palm and the back of the hand). Break the yarn, leaving about 15 inches (38 cm) of the background color. Use the Kitchener stitch to weave the ends together to finish the top of the mitten.

To work the Kitchener stitch, thread the yarn attached to the back needle (the needle that's away from you). Then, starting with the stitches on the front needle (the needle that's near to you), insert the tapestry needle into the first stitch of the front needle as if to purl, pull the yarn through but leave the stitch on the knitting needle.

Go to the back needle, being careful to take the yarn under the needle each time. Insert the tapestry needle into the first stitch as if to knit, pull the yarn through but leave the stitch on the knitting needle.

★ Insert the tapestry needle into the first stitch of the front needle as if to knit, then slip this stitch onto the tapestry needle. Insert the tapestry needle into the second stitch of the front needle as if to purl, pull the yarn through but leave the stitch on the knitting needle. Go to the back needle and insert the tapestry needle into the first stitch as if to purl. Take this stitch off and onto the tapestry needle. Put the tapestry needle through the second stitch of the back needle as if to knit. Pull the yarn through, but leave the second stitch on the knitting needle. ★

Repeat from ★ to ★ until all stitches are joined. Do not draw the yarn too tightly. The stitches should have the same tension as the knitted stitches. Fasten the end securely.

With the body complete, you're ready to finish the thumb. Slip the 21 (23); 25 (27); 31 (35) stitches of the thumb on the holder onto three double-pointed needles; 9 (10); 10 (11); 12 (14) on the first needle, 3; 5; 7 sts on the second needle, and 9 (10); 10 (11); 12 (14) on the third needle. Take the CC yarn and pick up one stitch in the CC seam stitch that is at the nearest side of the mitten. Place it on the end of the third needle.

Begin the first thumb round with MC yarn, and pick up one stitch in the center seam stitch. Place it on the first needle. Pick up one CC stitch following the center seam stitch, then follow the chart for the thumb until ready to decrease.

To decrease, begin with the first needle and k1 MC, k1 CC, ssk, then knit to the end of the needle following the pattern. Knit stitches on the second needle. On the third needle, knit to within 3 stitches of the end of the needle, k2tog, then knit the seam stitch.

Repeat the decreases until there are 8; 10; 12 stitches left. Transfer the stitches from each needle to two needles, with 4; 5; 6 sts on the front and back. Break the CC yarn, leaving a tail approximately 12 inches (30.5 cm) long for working the Kitchener Stitch as for the mitten top. Weave in all ends.

Blocking

Turn the mittens inside out. Place them in a bowl of water that is room temperature for at least 30 minutes. Gently squeeze the water out of the mittens, then roll them in a towel to remove the excess water. Dry them out of direct sunlight. When dry, turn right-side out and enjoy.

Working the Kitchener stitch.

Abbreviations

A

approx—approximately

B

beg—begin, beginning

br—bright

C

CC—contrasting color

cm—centimeter

co—cast on

cont—continue

D

dec—decrease, decreasing

dk —dark

dpn—double-pointed needles

E

eon—end of needle

G

g—grams

I

inc—increase, increasing

K

K—knit

K2tog—knit two together

L

lt—light

M

m—meters

MC—main color

med—medium

m1—make one

m1r—make one reverse

O

oz—ounce

P

P—purl

P2tog—purl two togehter

psso—pass slip stitch over

R

rnd(s)—round, rounds

S

sk—skip

skn—skein

sl—slip

sl st—slip stitch

ssk—slip, slip, knit (decrease one)

st(s)—stitch, stitches

st st stockinette stitch

T

tog

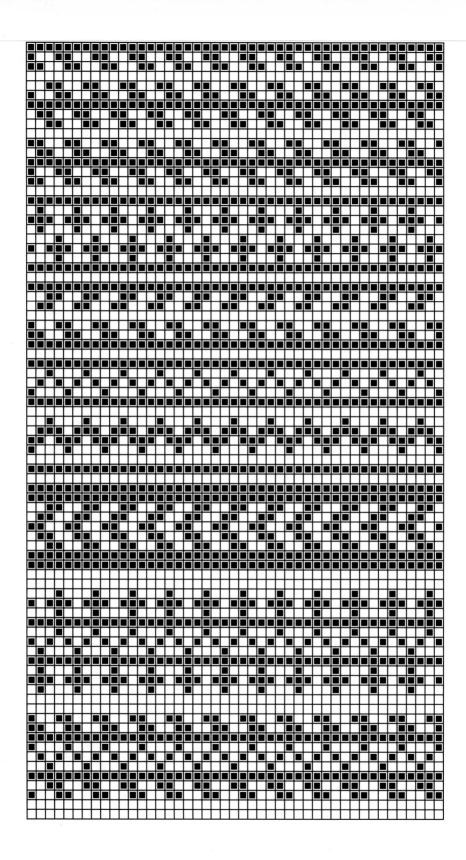

Basic Patterns

If you were given materials and asked to devise simple patterns, there would be a limited number you could create. In some of the mittens, several simple patterns are combined to create what at first looks like a complicated pattern, such as Mitten 1. Upon closer inspection, you'll see it's really two simple patterns that have been stacked together; this is the basic premise.

These patterns are the simplest system of Komi decoration. They are easy to understand and thus easy to follow while knitting. The patterns are used in borders and as reticulations. Some mittens are knit with several basic patterns stacked in borders, such as Mitten 2. Others use a variety of patterns that do not repeat, such as Mitten 3.

The basic borders were also interspersed with other borders, becoming a major portion of a mitten's hand or the leg of a stocking after the fancy patterning at the cuff was completed. Other simple reticulations were used that were more complex than the basic patterns, yet didn't fit within the other systems of patterning. Mitten 27 is an example of this, being a pattern reminiscent of Scandinavian knitting.

1

Though intricate looking, the overall pattern incorporates only two simple patterns, the cross and zigzag.

Size
Adult's Medium (Large)

Yarn
Brown Sheep Nature Spun Sport weight 100% Wool, 1¾ oz. (50 gr) = approx. 184 yds.(168 m) in #N 30 Nordic Blue (MC), #N 03 Grey Heather, and #N 87 Victorian Pink, 1 skein each.

If not available: Sport weight 100% wool, 1¾ oz. (50 gr) = approx. 185 yds.(168 m) in medium blue (MC), light grey, and medium pink, 1 skein each.

Needles
5, size 2 U.S. (2.75 mm, 12 U.K.) double-pointed needles or size to give gauge.

Gauge
16 sts and 18 rnds = 2" (5 cm) over two-color stockinette stitch worked in the round (all k).

Cast On
64 (72) sts

Cuff
Length: 3½" (9 cm), (3¾" (9.5 cm)).
K2, p2 rib all in med. blue.

Reticulation
4 sts x 12 rnds

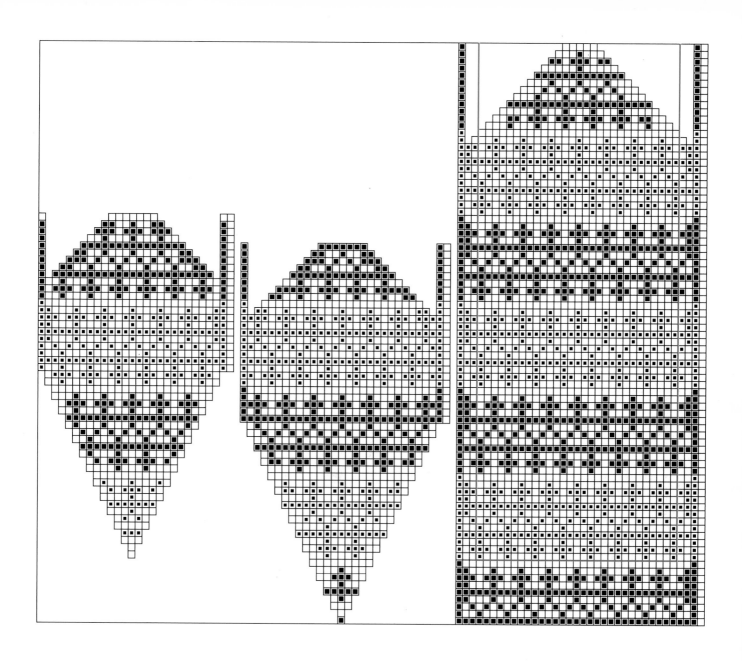

☐ MED. BLUE (MC)

■ LT. GREY

▪ MED. PINK

2

This mitten features a set of simple patterns that both repeat over four stitches. You can easily substitute colors to match a favorite jacket or use more colors from your yarn stash.

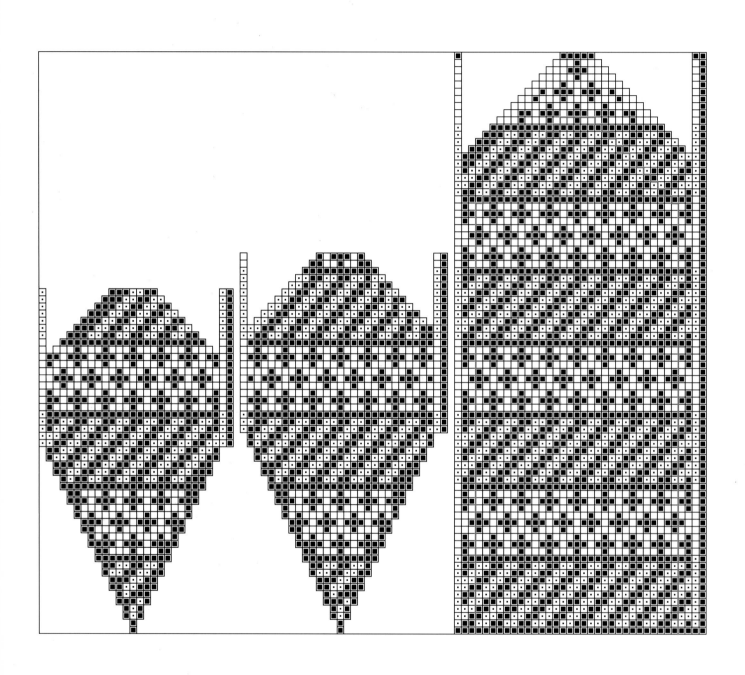

■ DK. PURPLE (MC)

☐ LT. YELLOW

• MED. GREY

Size

Adult's Medium (Large)

Yarn

Dale of Norway's Helio 100% wool, 1¾ oz.(50 g) = approx. 109 yds. (100. m),in #5264 Grape (MC), 2 skeins; #2314 Pale Yellow, and #7 Grey, 1 skein each.

If not available: 100% wool, 1¾ oz. (50g) = approx. 110 yds. (100 m) in dark purple (MC), 2 skeins; light yellow, and medium grey, 1 skein each.

Needles

5, size 2 U.S. (2.75 mm, 12 U.K.) double-pointed needles or size to give gauge.

Gauge

16 sts and 18 rnds = 2" (5 cm) over two-color stockinette stitch worked in the round (all k).

Cast On

64 (72) sts

Cuff

Length: 3½"(9 cm), (3¾" (9.5 cm)).

K2, p2 rib in stripes: 5 (7) rnds dk. purple, 3 rnds lt. yellow, 7 rnds dk. purple, 3 rnds med. grey, 5 (7) rnds dk. purple, 3 rnds lt. yellow, 5 (7) rnds dk. purple.

3

These easy patterns are satisfying to look at and a pleasure to work. The patterns are repeats of 1 st x 2 rnds, 4 sts x 4 rnds, and 2 sts x 2 rnds.

Size

Child's Medium (Large)

Yarn

Nordic Fiber Arts' Rauma Finnullgarn 2-ply 100% wool, 1¾ oz. (50 g) = approx. 178 yds. (163 m) in # 483 Turquoise (MC), #4986 Yellow, and #418 Red, 1 skein each.

If not available: 2-ply 100% wool, 1¾ oz. (50 g) = approx. 178 yds. (163 m) in dark turquoise (MC), yellow, and red, 1 skein each.

Needles

5, size 3 U.S. (3.25 mm, 10 U.K.) double-pointed needles or size to give gauge.

Gauge

16 sts and 18 rnds = 2" (5 cm) over two-color stockinette stitch worked in the round (all k).

Cast On

48 (56) sts

Cuff

Length: 2¾" (7cm), (3" (7.5)).

K2, p2 rib in dk. turquoise.

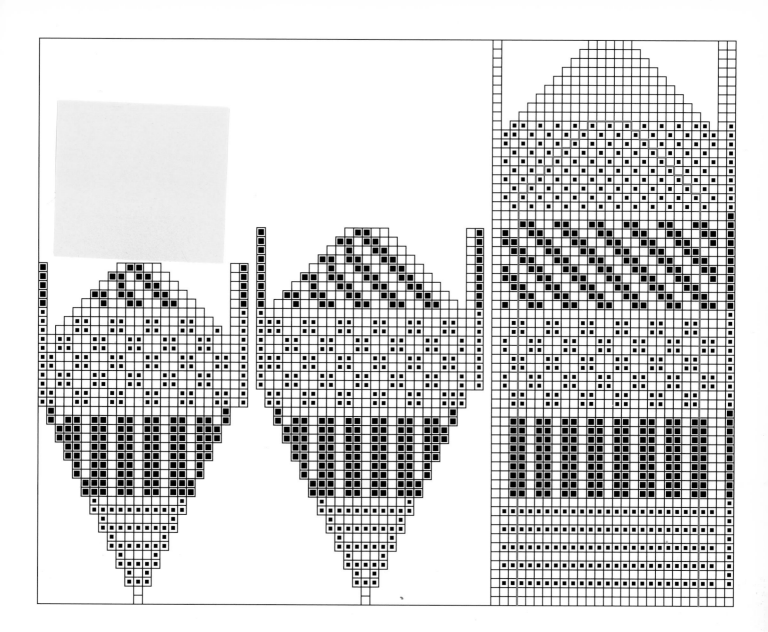

□ DK. TURQUOISE (MC)

■ YELLOW

■ RED

Septenary Borders

The Komi used these borders either consecutively or alternated them with borders created by the basic patterns. They are also used with wider borders on mittens or stockings. Septenary borders are created by isolating seven rows of larger reticulations. They follow the rules of reticulations (see page 55), and are symmetrical around a full three-stitch cross with two stitches above and two below.

The same pattern is used as light on dark as well as dark on light which sometimes gives quite a different look to the pattern. Most of the repeats in the borders are 18 stitches wide, although some are 12 or 24 stitches wide.

You can see patterns (a) and (b) in the chart are both seven rounds high; however, they do not follow the rules for creation that the other patterns do. This indicates that they may have been created later or brought to the area from another ethnic group.

4

With two different septenary borders and a repeating four-stitch border, this mitten is similar to Mitten 6. Each of the septenary borders is knit in a different color.

Size
Adult's Medium (Large)

Yarn
Brown Sheep Company's Nature Spun Fingering weight 100% Wool, 1¾ oz. (50 g) = approx. 310 yds. (284 m) in #880 Charcoal (MC), # 308 Sunburst Gold, #N 85 Peruvian Pink, and #N 65 Meadow Green, 1 skein each.

If not available: Fingering weight 100% Wool, 1¾ oz. (50 g) = approx. 310 yds. (284 m) in dark grey (MC), medium gold, dark rose, and medium grey green, 1 skein each.

Needles
5, size 1 U.S. (2.25 mm, 13 U.K.) double-pointed needles or size to give gauge.

Gauge
20 sts and 22 rnds = 2" (5 cm) over two-color stockinette stitch worked in the round (all k).

Cast On
80 (92) sts

Cuff
Length: 3½"(9 cm), (3¾" (9.5 cm)).
K2, p2 rib in dk. grey.

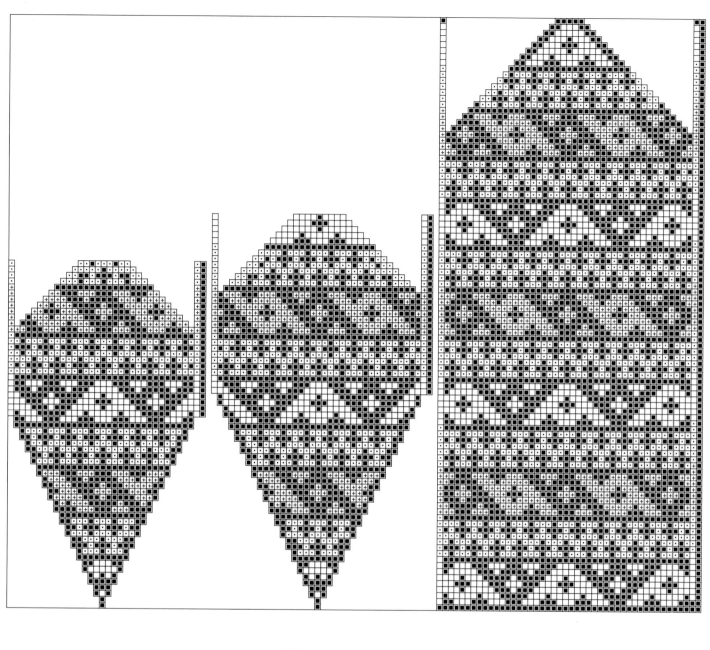

■ DK. GREY (MC)

+ MED. GOLD

☐ DK. ROSE

• MED. GREY GREEN

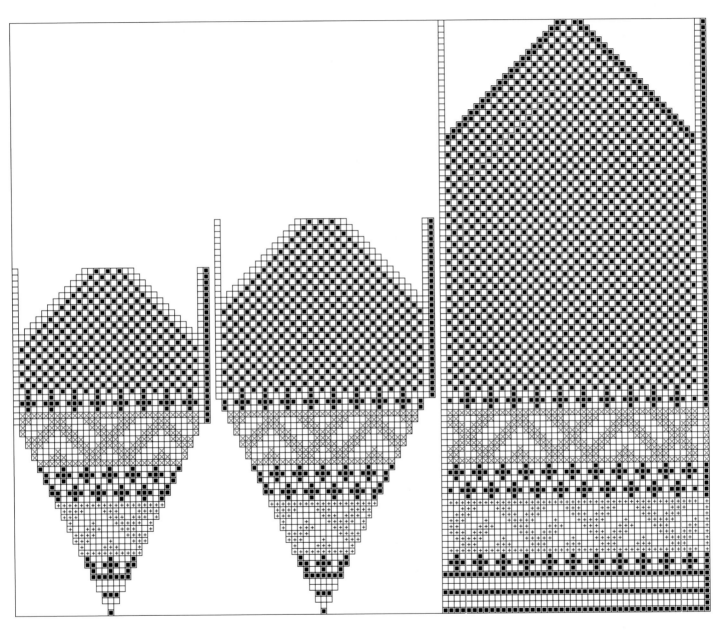

□ WHITE

■ BLACK (MC)

⊠ GREEN (MC)

+ RED (MC)

*T*wo septenary borders, a four-stitch cross pattern, stripes, and a 2 sts x 2 rnd checkerboard make this a pleasing pattern.

Size

Adult's Medium (Large)

Yarn

Helmi Vuorelma Oy Satakieli 2-ply 100% wool, 3½ oz. (100 g) = approx. 357 yds. (326 m) in White, and Black (MC), 1 skein each; Red (MC), and Green (MC). ½ skein each.

If not available: 2-ply 100% wool, 3½ oz. (100 g) = approx. 357 yds. (326 m) in white, and black (MC), 1 skein each; red, and green. ½ skein each.

Needles

5, size 0 U.S.(2 mm, 14 U.K.) double-pointed needles or size to give gauge.

Gauge

20 sts and 22 rnds = 2" (5 cm) over two-color stockinette stitch worked in the round (all k).

Cast On

80 (92) sts

Cuff

Length: 3½" (9 cm), (3-3/4" (9.5 cm)). K2, p2 rib in black.

6

Like Mitten 4, this mitten's design combines two different septenary borders with a repeating four-stitch border. To my eye, the four-stitch border resembles arrowheads or a vine.

Size

Child's Medium (Large)

Yarn

Nordic Fiber Arts' Rauma Finnullgarn 2-ply 100% wool, 1¾ oz (50 g) = approx. 178 yds. in #4887 Green (MC), #4986 Yellow, and #4686 Pink, 1 skein each.

If not available: 2-ply 100% wool, 1¾ oz (50 g) = approx. 178 yds. in green (MC), yellow, and pink, 1 skein each.

Needles

5, size 3 U.S. (3.25 mm, 10 U.K.) double-pointed needles or size to give gauge.

Gauge

16 sts and 18 rnds = 2" (5 cm) over two-color stockinette stitch worked in the round (all k).

Cast On

48 (56) sts

Cuff

Length: 3" (5 cm), (3" (5 cm)).

Corrugated rib knit green, purl yellow and pink. Work 5 (7) rnds yellow, 5 rnds pink, 5 rnds yellow, 5 rnds pink, 5 (7) rnds yellow.

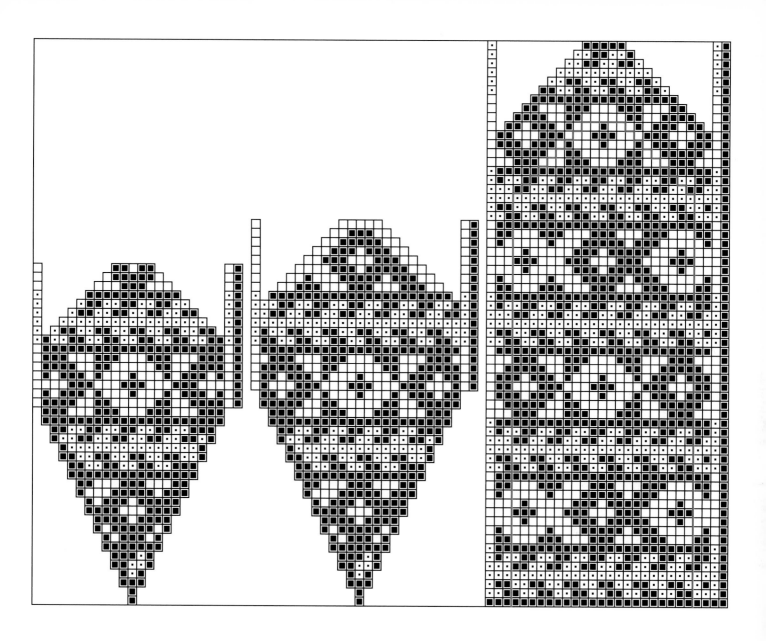

■ GREEN (MC)

☐ YELLOW

· PINK

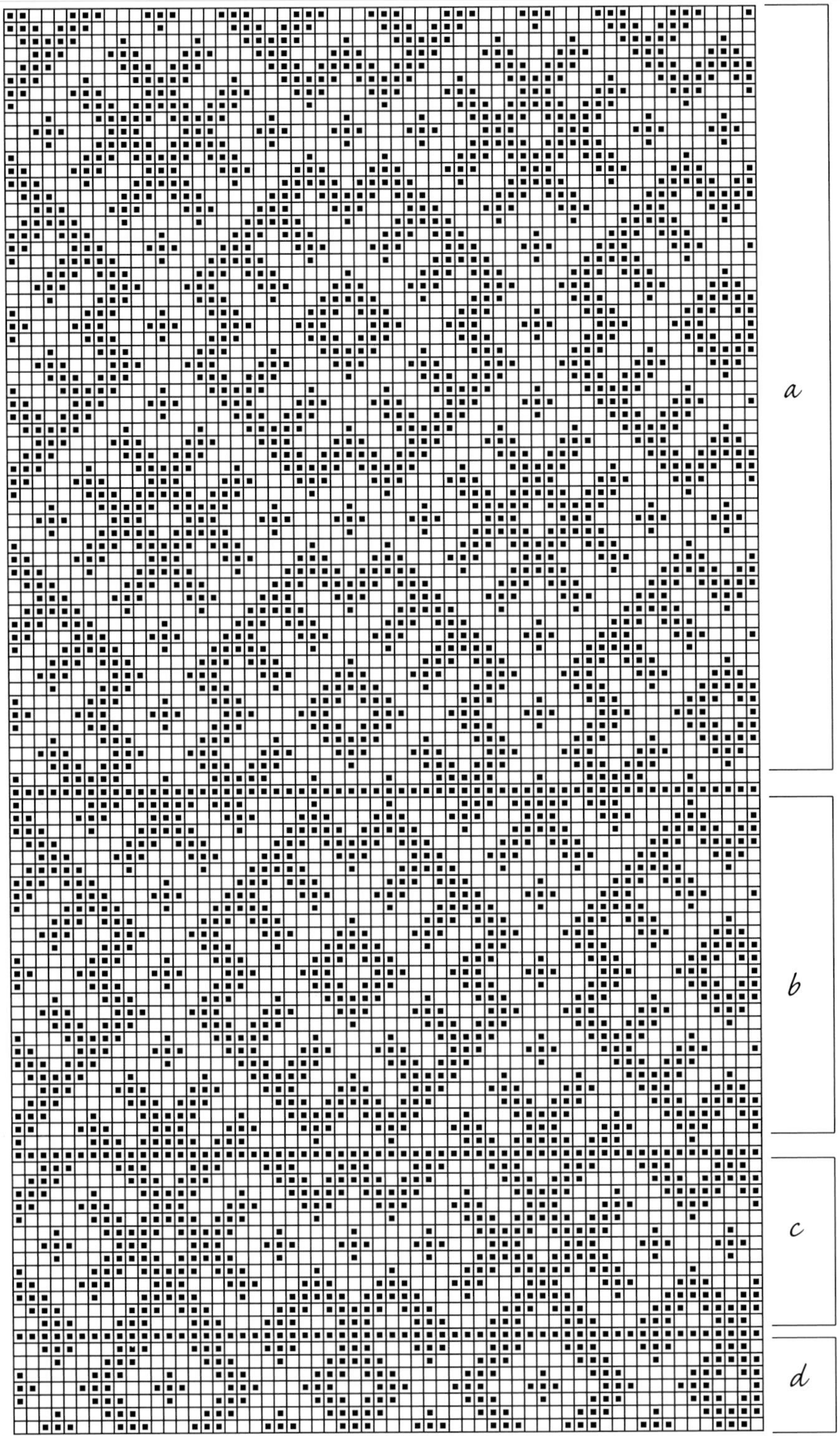
a
b
c
d

Wide Borders

These patterns can be used as complete wide borders, allover patterns, septenary borders, or borders combined with basic patterns. The chart provides an example of how a pattern can be worked as (a) a reticulation; (b) a wide border 27 rounds high; (c) a border 13 rounds high; and (d) a septenary border. This particular pattern is used for Mitten 10.

7

Some patterns seem to be only borders. After much thought, I determined this border, though the largest, doesn't lend itself to becoming a reticulation.

Size
Adult's Medium (Large)

Yarn
Brown Sheep Company's Nature Spun Fingering weight 100% Wool, 1¾ oz. (50 g) = approx. 310 yds. (284 m) in #N 33 Tile Blue, #N 42 Royal Purple (MC), #N 85 Peruvian Pink (MC), and #N 78 Turquoise Wonder, 1 skein each.

If not available: Fingering weight 100% Wool, 1¾ oz. (50 g) = approx. 310 yds. (284 m) in light grey blue, deep purple (MC), bright rose (MC), and dark turquoise, 1 skein each.

Needles
5, size 1 U.S.(2.25 mm, 13 U.K.) double-pointed needles or size to give gauge.

Gauge
20 sts and 22 rnds = 2" (5 cm) over two-color stockinette stitch worked in the round (all k).

Cast On
80 (92) sts

Cuff
Length: 3½"(9 cm), (3¾" (9.5 cm)).
Corrugated rib knit purple, purl rose and dk.turquoise 6 (7) rnds each, repeat for length.

Reticulation
60 sts x 49 rnds

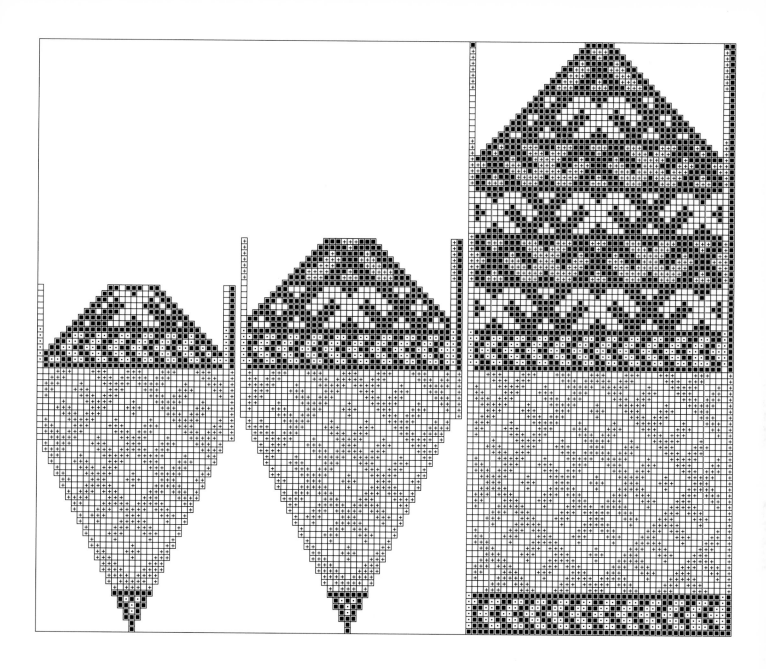

- ·   LT. GREY BLUE

■   PURPLE (MC)

+   BR. ROSE (MC)

   DK. TURQUOISE

8

By centering two patterns with different repeats, I was able to devise a larger pattern where the two work harmoniously together.

Size
Adult's Medium (Large)

Yarn
Brown Sheep Company's Nature Spun Fingering weight 100% Wool, 1¾ oz. (50 g) = approx. 310 yards (284 m) in #710 Bark Cloth (MC), #N 17 French Clay, and #720 Ash, 1 skein each.

If not available: Fingering weight 100% wool, 1¾ oz. (50 g) = approx. 310 yards (284 m) in red brown (MC), red gold, and light tan, 1 skein each.

Needles
5, size 1 U.S. (2.25 mm, 13 U.K.) double-pointed needles or size to give gauge.

Gauge
20 sts and 22 rnds = 2" (5 cm) over two-color stockinette stitch worked in the round (all k).

Cast On
80 (92) sts

Cuff
Length: Work cuff from the chart.

Cast on twisted edge with two colors using lt. tan and red brown. Work the chart for the cuff until the first break in pattern, then ¾" (2 cm) of k2, p2 rib in red brown before working the body of the mitten.

Reticulation
36 sts x 36 rnds; 24 sts x 24 rnds

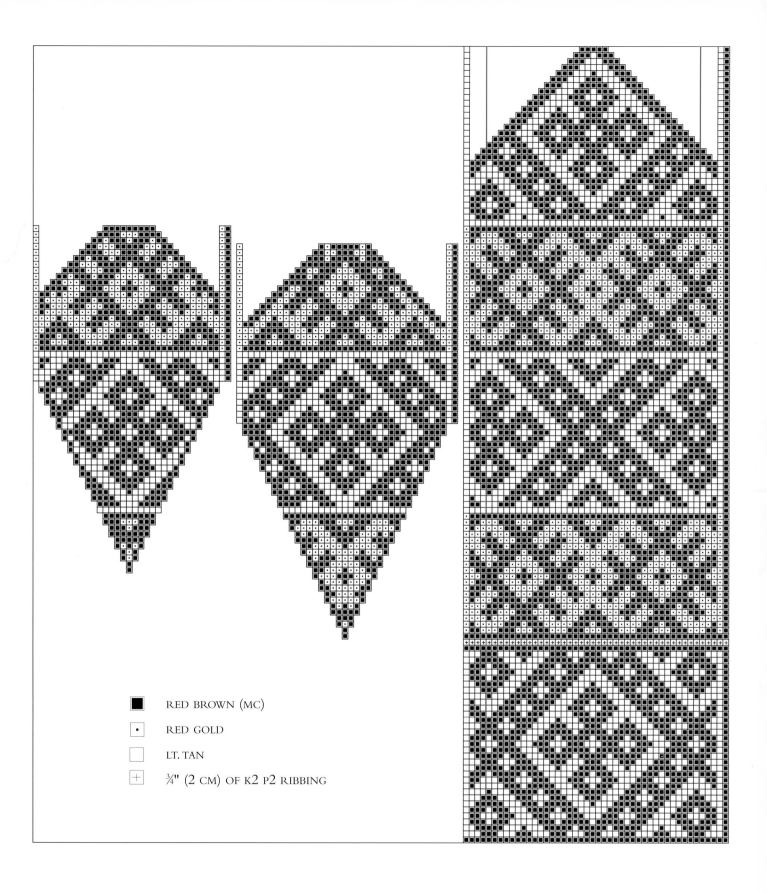

■ RED BROWN (MC)

· RED GOLD

☐ LT. TAN

⊞ ¾" (2 CM) OF K2 P2 RIBBING

9

■ BROWN (MC)

□ GOLD

▫ ORANGE

Once part of an impressive reticulation, the pattern creates an attractive border.

Size
Adult's Medium (Large)

Yarn
Nordic Fiber Arts' Rauma Finnullgarn 2-ply 100% Wool, 1¾ oz. (50 g) = approx. 178 yds. in #422 Brown (MC), 2 skeins; #460 Orange and #450 Yellow, 1 skein each.

If not available: 2-ply 100% wool, 1¾ oz. (50 g) = approx. 178 yds. in brown (MC), 2 skeins; orange and gold, 1 skein each.

Needles
5, size 3 U.S. (3.25 mm, 10 U.K.) double-pointed needles or size to give gauge.

Gauge
16 sts and 18 rnds = 2" (5 cm) over two-color stockinette stitch worked in the round (all k).

Cast On
64 (72) sts

Cuff
Length: 3½ " (9 cm) (3¾ " (9.5 cm)).

Corrugated rib knit brown, purl orange.

Reticulation
30 sts x 30 rnds

10

*T*he reticulation combines two of the most popularly used motifs, the 2 x and the 3 x, one light on dark and the other dark on light. The frame of dark stitches around the 3 x creates a beautiful motif for the border of the mitten.

size
Adult's Medium (Large)

Yarn
Brown Sheep Company's Nature Spun Fingering weight 100% Wool, 1¾ oz (50 g) = approx. 310 yds. (284 m) in #308 Sunburst Gold, #N 17 French Clay, #N 39 Navy Nite (MC), 1 skein each.

If not available: Fingering weight 100% wool, 1¾ oz (50 g) = approx. 310 yds. (284 m) in gold, red gold, navy blue (MC), 1 skein each.

Needles
5, size 1 U.S. (2.25 mm, 13 U.K.) double-pointed needles or size to give gauge.

Gauge
20 sts and 22 rounds = 2" (5 cm) over two-color stockinette stitch worked in the round (all k).

Cast On
80 (92) sts

Cuff
Length: Work k1, p1 rib for ½" (1.5 cm) in navy blue. Work the chart for the cuff until the first break in pattern, then ¾" (2 cm) of k2, p2 rib in navy blue before working the body of the mitten. If you prefer, you may substitute a ribbed cuff of 3½" (9 cm), (3¾" (9.5 cm)).

Reticulation
30 sts x 30 rnds

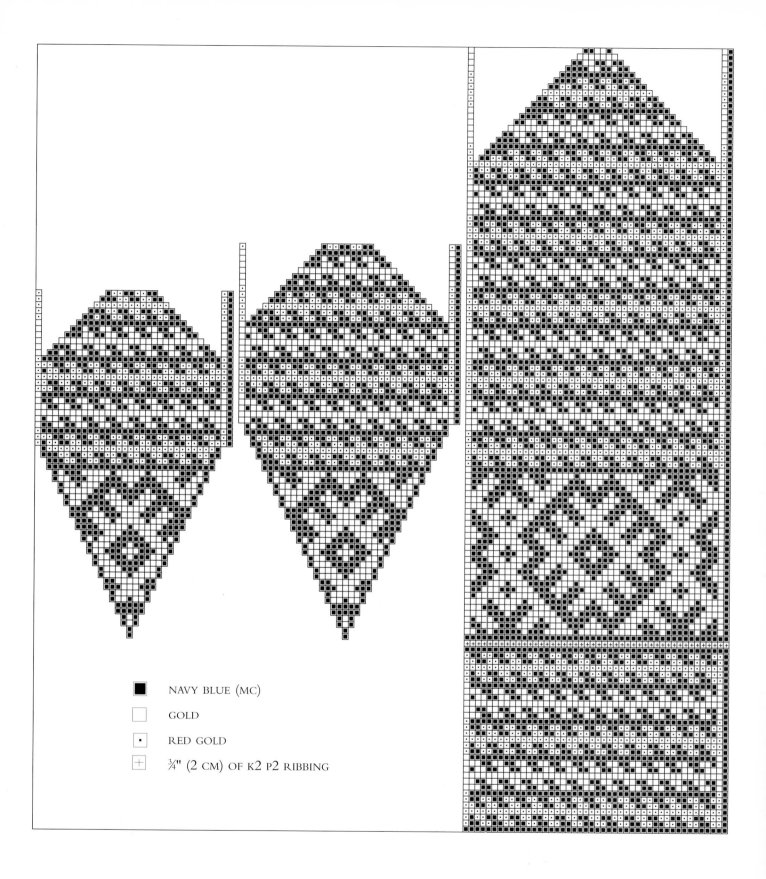

■ NAVY BLUE (MC)

□ GOLD

· RED GOLD

⊞ ¾" (2 CM) OF K2 P2 RIBBING

11

One large border combined with three easier patterns creates this design. You'll find a Komi-style pattern of four rounds, and two patterns worked with four-stitch repeats.

Size
Adult's Medium (Large)

Yarn
Brown Sheep Company's Nature Spun Fingering weight 100% Wool, 1¾ oz.(50 g) = approx. 310 yds. (284 m) in #N 76 Antique Turquoise, #N 21 Mallard (MC), and #N 48 Scarlet (MC), 1 skein each.

If not available: Fingering weight 100% wool, 1¾ oz.(50 g) = approx. 310 yds. (284 m) in medium turquoise, dark blue green (MC), medium red, 1 skein each.

Needles
5, size 1 U.S.(2.25 mm, 13 U.K.) double-pointed needles or size to give gauge.

Gauge
20 sts and 22 rnds = 2" (5 cm) over two-color stockinette stitch worked in the round (all k).

Cast On
80 (92) sts

Cuff
Length: 3½"(9 cm), (3¾"(9.5 cm)).

Corrugated rib knit dk. blue green, purl med. red.

Reticulation
42 sts X 42 rnds

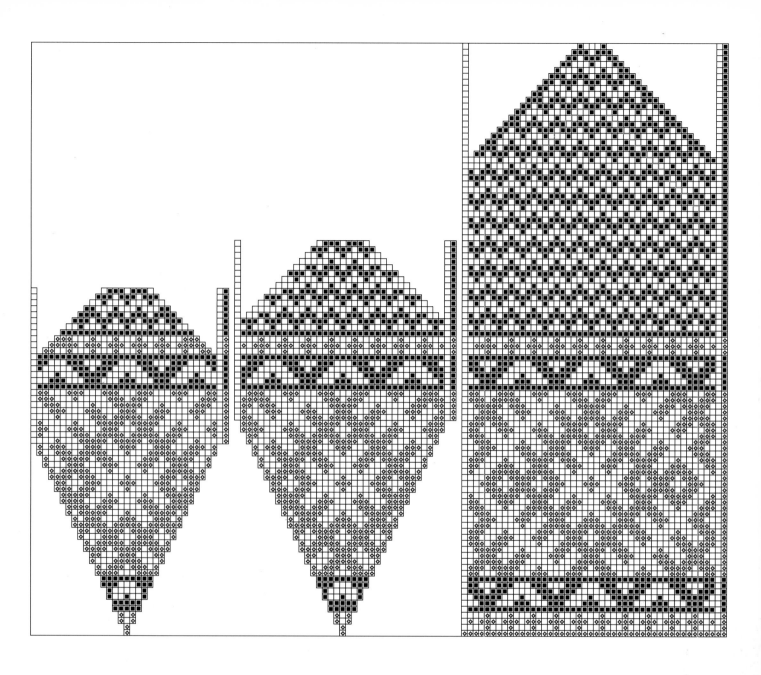

□ MED. TURQUOISE

■ DK. BLUE GREEN (MC)

◇ MED. RED (MC)

12

*T*he core of this pattern is a
star-type motif. At 42 sts x
54 rnds it's one of the
largest reticulations.

Size
Adult's Medium (Large)

Yarn
Brown Sheep Company's Nature Spun
Fingering weight 100% Wool, 1¾
oz.(50 g) = approx. 310 yds. (284 m) in
#720 Ash (MC), #N 72 Metropolis
Turquoise, and #N 42 Royal Purple, 1
skein each.

If not available: Fingering-weight 100%
wool, 1¾ oz. (50 g) = approx. 310 yds.
(284 m) in light tan (MC), medium
turquoise, and dark purple, 1 skein each.

Needles
5, size 1 U.S. (2.25 mm, 13 U.K.) double-
pointed needles or size to give gauge.

Gauge
20 sts and 22 rnds = 2" (5 cm) over
two-color stockinette stitch worked in
the round (all k).

Cast On
80 (92) sts

Cuff
Length: 3½"(9 cm),(3¾"(9.5 cm)).

Corrugated rib knit lt. tan, purl dk.
purple and med.turquoise worked in 6-
rnd stripes.

Reticulation
42 sts x 54 rnds

☐ LT. TAN (MC)

■ MED. TURQUOISE

▪ DK. PURPLE

B

When expanded into a reticulation, this pattern has only a horizontal axis. It makes a pleasing allover design.

If not available: 2-ply 100% wool, 1¾ oz (50 g) = approx. 178 yds. (163 m) in burgundy (MC), dark rose (MC), and medium blue, 1 skein each.

Needles
5, size 3 U.S. (3.25 mm, 10 U.K.) double-pointed needles or size to give gauge.

Gauge
16 sts and 18 rnds – 2" (5 cm) over two-color stockinette stitch worked in the round (all k).

Size
Adult's Medium (Large)

Cast On
64 (72)

Yarn
Nordic Fiber Arts' Raumagarn Finnullgarn 2-ply 100% Wool, 1¾ oz (50 g) = approx. 178 yds. (163 m) in #480 Burgundy (MC), #490 Dark Rose (MC), and #451 Blue, 1 skein each.

Cuff
Length: 3½" (9 cm), (3¾" (9.5 cm)).
k2 p2 rib in burgundy.

■ BURGUNDY (MC)

□ DK. ROSE (MC)

• MED. BLUE

14

I copied this pattern from a woven belt from the Komi Republic that was given to me. Although the actual belt pattern is a border, it can be repeated in a variety of ways to create a reticulation. The simple reticulation above the border is a repeat of 6 sts X 4 rnds.

Size
Child's Medium (Large)

Yarn
Nordic Fiber Arts' Rauma Finnullgarn 2-ply 100% Wool, 1¾ oz. (50 g) = approx. 178 yds. (163 m) in #436 Black (MC), #437 Blue, and #403 Grey, 1 skein each.

If not available: 2-ply 100% wool, 1¾ oz. (50 g) = approx. 178 yds. (163 m) in black (MC), blue, and light grey, 1 skein each.

Needles
5, size 3 U.S. (3.25 mm, 10 U.K.) double-pointed needles or size to give gauge.

Gauge
16 sts and 18 rnds = 2" (5 cm) over two-color stockinette stitch worked in the round (all k).

Cast On
48 (56) sts

Cuff
Length: 2¾" (7 cm), (3" (7.5 cm)).
Corrugated rib knit black, purl blue.

Reticulation
24 sts x 18 rnds

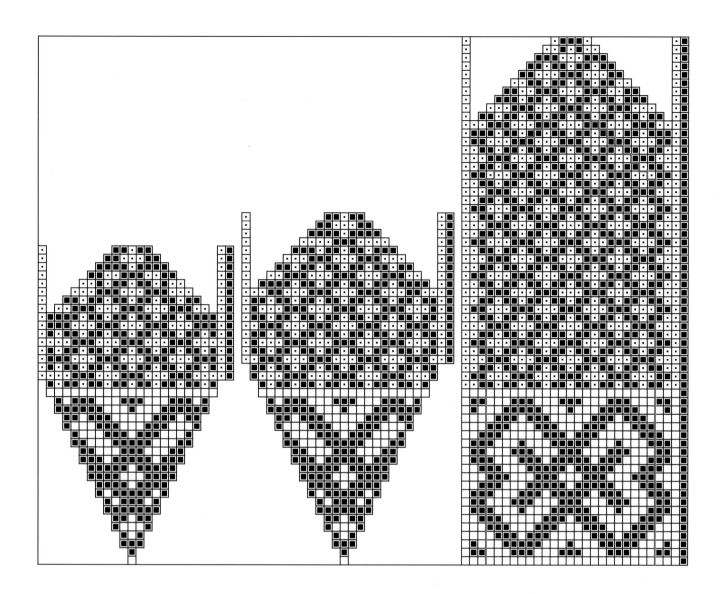

■ BLACK (MC)

· BLUE

□ LT. GREY

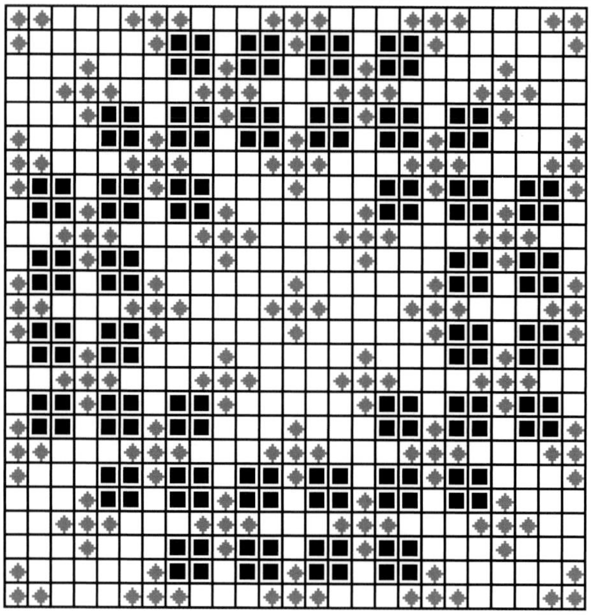

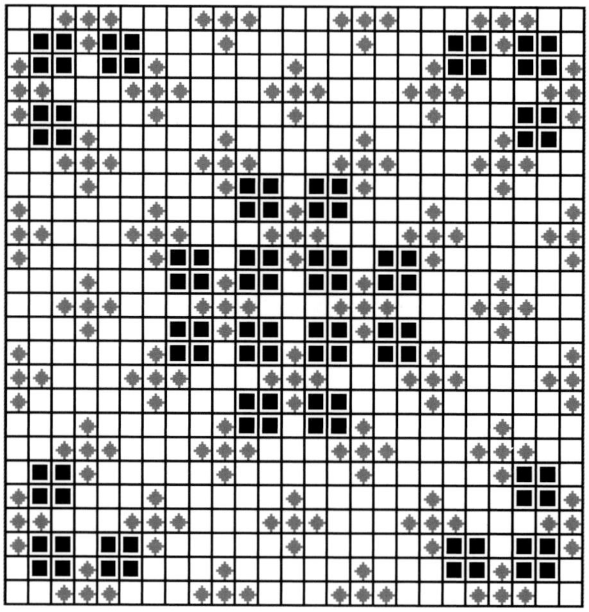

Reticulations

These patterns are the core of the magic of the Komi patterning. Reticulations follow four rules:

1) The fundamental pattern is the crosses that are repeated, giving the whole fundamental pattern a repeat of 6 sts x 6 rnds. This results in every third row being three dark and three light stitches.
2) The working patterns are created with knitted color repeats of 1, 3, 5 only.
3) The lines of the design are three stitches wide.
4) The diagonal pattern is aligned on the vertical and horizontal axis. This can be the same pattern or two different alternating patterns. Mittens 10 and 29 are examples of how patterns can alternate.

The chart shows how a pattern of 24 sts X 24 rnd would be created. This pattern is symmetrical horizontally as well as vertically, and all the motifs are the same. A pattern line on the diagonal creates stronger knitted fabric than a vertical line. This works well with the technique of knitting, since the pattern moves diagonally across the fabric allowing the floats across the back to also travel. This makes for a flatter fabric and one whose stitch shape becomes almost square, rather than the short, wide stitch of a single-color stockinette stitch.

This style of pattern is used as a reticulation, but some have been adapted for use as borders by selecting a portion of the allover design. A favorite is the seven-row, or septenary, border which follows most of the rules of the reticulations, but has only one axis. Borders can also be 10, 13, or more stitches wide. For symmetry, the wider borders are 3 X +1 stitches wide and start and end with the three dark, three light row. However, the wider borders do not have to be symmetrical.

When working with the reticulations, you'll find it's easy to combine the patterns into beautiful designs because of their appealing symmetry. As examples, Mitten 15 uses four patterns, a simple 6 x 6, two reticulations, and a basic pattern on the thumb; Mitten 27 uses a simple 6 x 8 pattern with a basic on the thumb and tip. Always remember to center the patterns on the piece and be sure to relate the patterns to each other when stacking your borders.

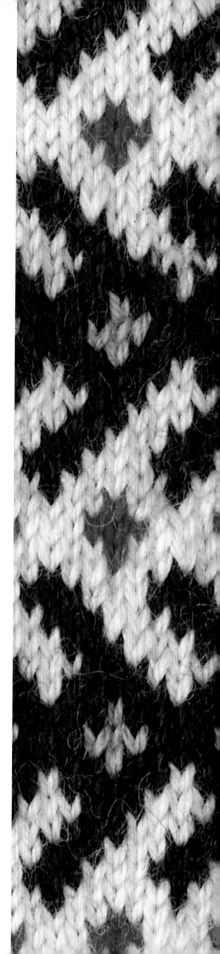

15

It's always fun to see how a collection of Komi patterns can look together. I designed this mitten using three different patterns for the palm, thumb, and back; the chart on the right corresponds to the back, the chart on the left to the palm (or reverse as you please!). The main reticulation (the chart on the right) is a 24 sts x 24 rnds pattern, with a base-cross pattern on the chart on the left. The thumb is a 2 st x 2 rnd checkerboard.

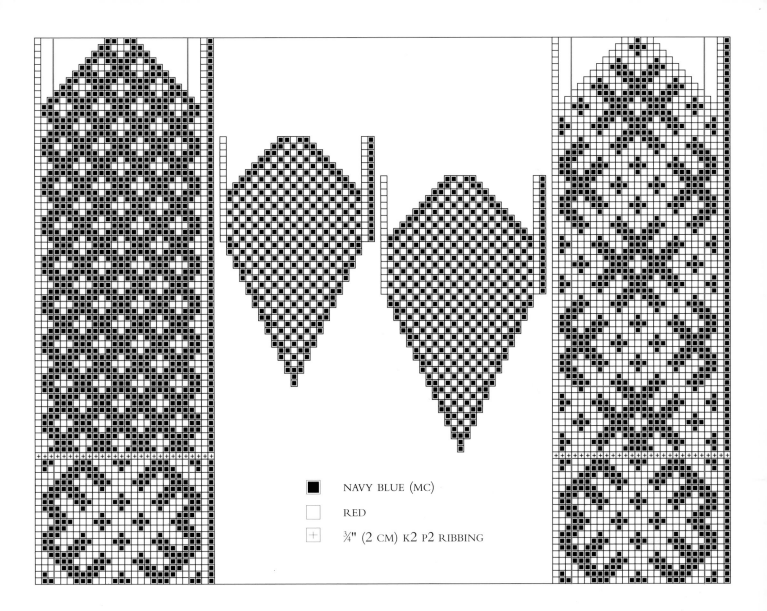

■		NAVY BLUE (MC)
□		RED
+		¾" (2 CM) K2 P2 RIBBING

Size
Child's Medium (Large)

Yarn
Nordic Fiber Arts' Rauma Finnullgarn 2-ply 100% Wool, 1¾ oz. (50 g) = approx. 178 yds. (163 m) in #449 Navy Blue (MC) and #439 Cool Red, 1 skein each.

If not available: 2-ply 100% wool, 1¾ oz. (50 g) = approx. 178 yds. (163 m) in navy blue (MC) and red, 1 skein each.

Needles
5, size 3 U.S. (3.25 mm, 10 U.K.) double-pointed needles or size to give gauge.

Gauge
16 sts and 18 rnds = 2" (5 cm) over two-color stockinette stitch worked in the round (all k).

Cast On
48 (56) sts

Cuff
Length: Work from the chart.

Cast on twisted edge with two colors. Work the chart for the cuff until the first break in the pattern, then ¾" (2 cm) k 2, p 2 rib in navy blue before working the body of the mitten.

Reticulation
24 sts x 24 rnds

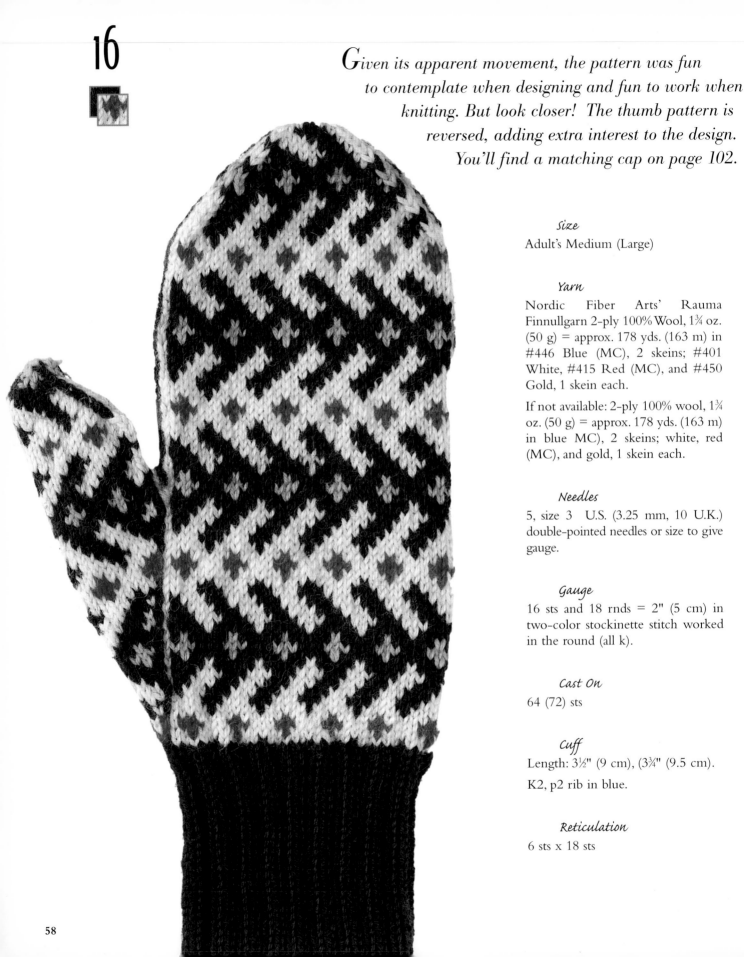

16

Given its apparent movement, the pattern was fun to contemplate when designing and fun to work when knitting. But look closer! The thumb pattern is reversed, adding extra interest to the design. You'll find a matching cap on page 102.

You'll find a matching cap on page 102.

Size
Adult's Medium (Large)

Yarn
Nordic Fiber Arts' Rauma Finnullgarn 2-ply 100% Wool, 1¾ oz. (50 g) = approx. 178 yds. (163 m) in #446 Blue (MC), 2 skeins; #401 White, #415 Red (MC), and #450 Gold, 1 skein each.

If not available: 2-ply 100% wool, 1¾ oz. (50 g) = approx. 178 yds. (163 m) in blue MC), 2 skeins; white, red (MC), and gold, 1 skein each.

Needles
5, size 3 U.S. (3.25 mm, 10 U.K.) double-pointed needles or size to give gauge.

Gauge
16 sts and 18 rnds = 2" (5 cm) in two-color stockinette stitch worked in the round (all k).

Cast On
64 (72) sts

Cuff
Length: 3½" (9 cm), (3¾" (9.5 cm).
K2, p2 rib in blue.

Reticulation
6 sts x 18 sts

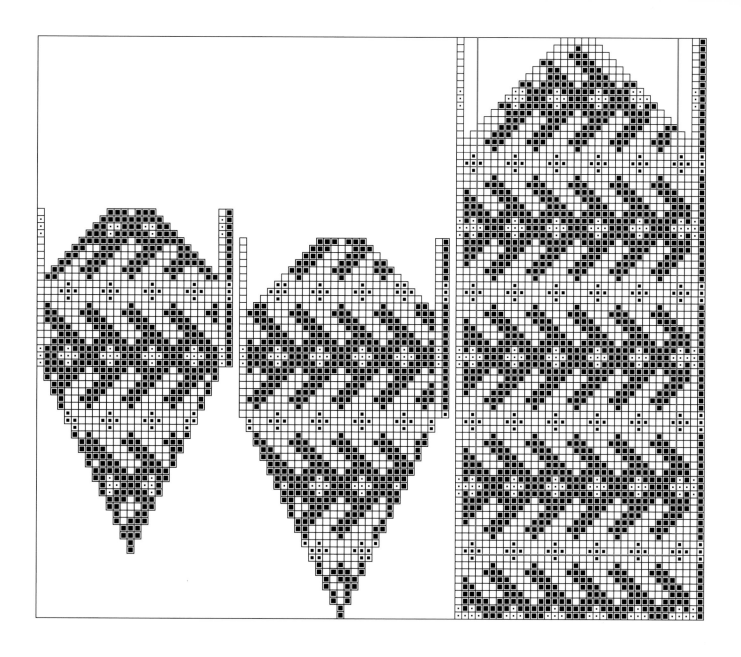

■   BLUE (MC)

□   WHITE

▪   RED (MC)

·   GOLD

17

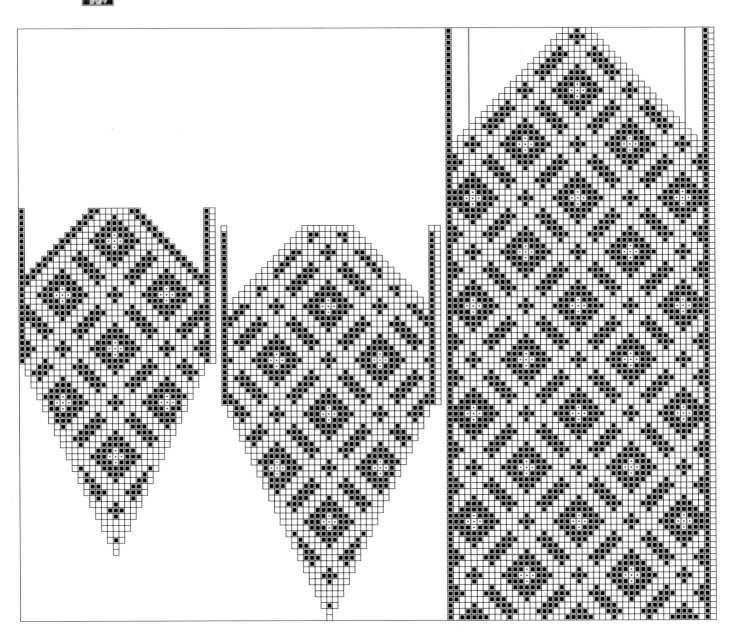

MED. BLUE (MC)

■ DK. BLUE

• CREAM

The 18 sts x 18 rnds reticulation has cream-colored centers in the middle of the dark blue squares. To avoid carrying the cream color over 15 stitches, substitute the lighter blue for the cream color, making a two-color reticulation. Then make a duplicate stitch in the cream color, using approximately a 12-inch (30.5 cm) length for each center.

Size
Adult's Medium (Large)

Yarn
Brown Sheep Company's Nature Spun Fingering-Weight 100% Wool, 1¾ oz. (50 g) = approx. 310 yds. (283 m) #117 Winter Blue (MC), #110 Blueberry, and #750 White Port, 1 skein each.

If not available: Fingering-weight 100% wool, 1¾ oz. (50 g) = approx. 310 yds. (283 m) medium blue (MC), dark blue, and cream, 1 skein each.

Needles
5, size 1 U.S. (2.25 mm, 13 U.K.) double-pointed needles or size to give gauge.

Gauge
20 sts and 22 rnds = 2" (5 cm) over two-color stockinette stitch worked in the round (all k).

Cast On
80 (92) sts

Cuff
Length: 3½" (9 cm), (3¾"(9.5 cm)).
Corrugated rib knit med. blue, purl dk. blue.

Reticulation
18 sts x 18 rnds

Though it looks large, the reticulation at 24 sts x 24 rnds is one of the smaller repeats, being made from two different elements.

Size
Adult's Medium (Large)

Yarn
Nordic Fiber Arts' Rauma Finnullgarn 2-ply 100% Wool, 1¾ oz. (50 g) = approx. 178 yds. (163 m) in #403 Grey and #418 Red (MC), 1 skein each.

If not available: 2-ply 100% wool, 1¾ oz. (50 g) = approx. 178 yds. (163 m) in light grey and red (MC), 1 skein each.

Needles
5, size 3 U.S. (3.25 mm, 10 U.K.) double-pointed needles or size to give gauge.

Gauge
16 sts and 18 rnds = 2" (5 cm) over two-color stockinette stitch worked in the round (all k).

Cast On
64 (72) sts

Cuff
Length: 3½" (9 cm), (3¾" (9.5 cm)).

Corrugated rib knit lt. grey, purl red.

Reticulation
24 sts x 24 rnds

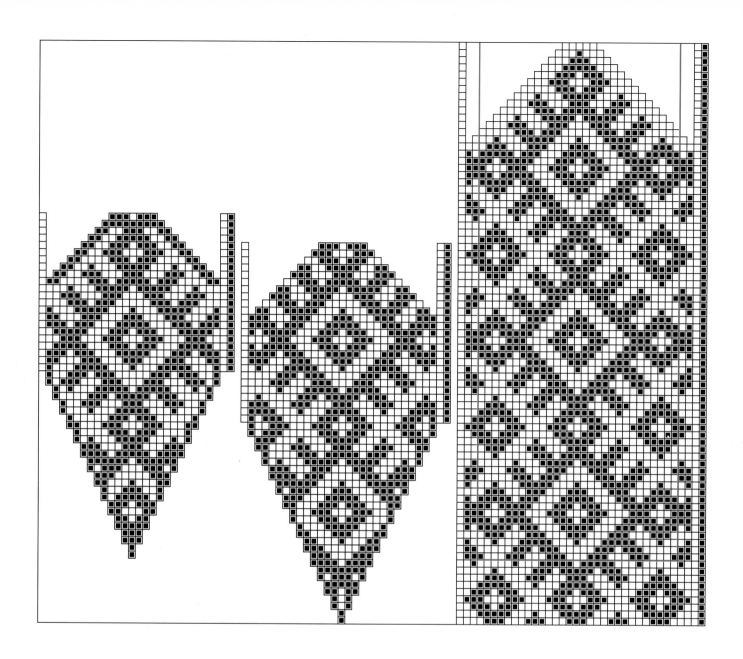

☐ LT GREY

■ RED (MC)

19

☐	LT. YELLOW
■	ROYAL BLUE (MC)
◆	BLUE VIOLET (MC)
◇	BLUE GREEN (MC)
+	¾" (2 CM) K2 P2 RIBBING

For this mitten I've included a color reverse on the left side of the chart; the right side of the chart is as knit. You can see how reversing light and dark can easily change the look of a mitten. You'll find this 12 sts x 12 rnds reticulation is one of the easier ones to work.

Size
Child's Medium (Large)

Yarn
Nordic Fiber Arts' Rauma Finnullgarn 2-ply 100% Wool, 1¾ oz. (50 g) = approx. 178 yds. (163 m) in #4986 Yellow, #467 Blue (MC), #448 Blue Violet (MC), and #484 Blue Green, 1 skein each.

If not available: 2-ply 100% wool, 1¾ oz. (50 g) = approx. 178 yds. (163 m) in light yellow, royal blue (MC), blue violet (MC), and blue green, 1 skein each.

Needles
5, size 3 U.S. (3.25 mm, 10 U.K.) double-pointed needles or size to give gauge.

Gauge
16 sts and 18 rnds = 2" (5 cm) over two-color stockinette stitch worked in the round (all k).

Cast On
48 (56) sts

Cuff
Length: Work from the chart.

Cast on twisted edge with two colors using lt. yellow and blue violet. Work the chart for the cuff until the first break in the pattern, then ¾" (2 cm) of k2, p2 rib in blue violet before working the body of the mitten.

Reticulation
12 sts x 12 rnds

20

One major difference in this pattern is the longer length of the lines or hooks from the diamonds that give it a look similar to patterns of the North American Eskimos. This pattern is one pattern repeated on both axes.

Size
Adult's Medium (Large)

Yarn
Brown Sheep Company's Nature Spun Fingering-Weight 100% Wool, 1¾ oz. (50 g) = approx. 310 yds (283 m) in #N 42 Royal Purple (MC), #N 62 Amethyst (MC), #N 43 Machu Picchu Purple (MC), #N 80 Mountain Purple (MC), and #N 20 Arctic Moss, 1 skein each.

If not available: Fingering-weight 100% wool, 1¾ oz. (50 g) = approx. 310 yds (283 m) in dark purple (MC), medium purple (MC), dark rose (MC), light purple (MC), and light sage green, 1 skein each.

Needles
5, size 1 U.S. (2.25 mm, 13 U.K.) double-pointed needles or size to give gauge.

Gauge
20 sts and 22 rnds = 2" (5 cm) over two-color stockinette stitch worked in the round (all k).

Cast On
80 (92) sts

Cuff
Length: 3½" (9 cm), (3¾" (9.5 cm)).
Corrugated rib knit grey green, purl purple colors worked in 3-rnd stripes.

Reticulation
48 sts x 72 rnds

	LT. SAGE GREEN
◆	DK. PURPLE (MC)
◇	MED. PURPLE (MC)
▪	DK. ROSE (MC)
■	LT. PURPLE (MC)

21

Another pleasing star-type pattern.

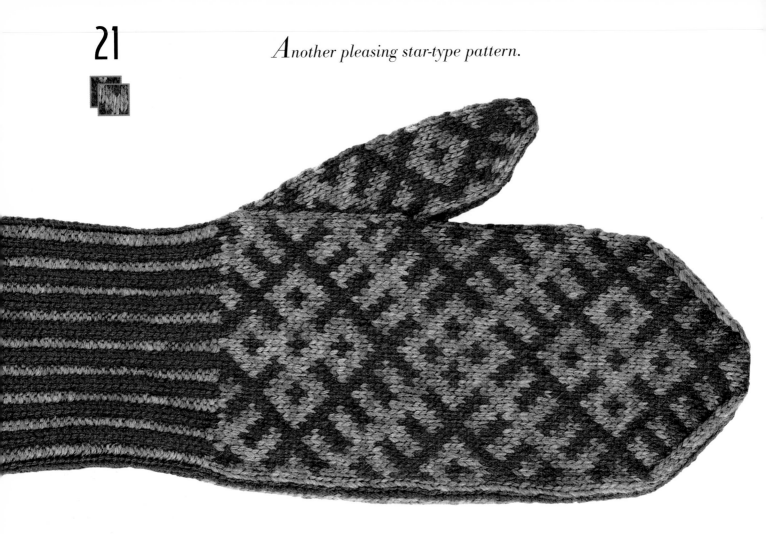

Size

Adult's Medium (Large)

Yarn

Brown Sheep Company's Nature Spun Sport weight 100% Wool, 1¾ oz. (50 g) = approx. 184 yds. (168 m) in #N 40 Grape Harvest (MC), 1 skein; Sport weight 100% wool, 2 oz. (56 g) = approx. 210 yds. (192 m) in rose/grey/green variegated, 1 skein.

If not available: Sport weight 100% wool, 1¾ oz. (50 g) = approx. 184 yds. (168 m) in burgundy (MC), 1 skein; Sport weight 100 % wool, 2 oz (56 g) = approx. 210 yds. (192 m) in rose/grey/ green variegated, 1 skein.

Needles

5, size 2 U.S. (2.75 mm, 12 U.K) double-pointed needles or size to give gauge.

Gauge

16 sts and 18 rnds = 2" (5 cm) over two-color stockinette stitch worked in the round (all k).

Cast On

64 (72) sts

Cuff

Length: 3½" (9 cm), (3¾"(9.5 cm)).

Corrugated rib knit burgundy, purl variegated.

Reticulation

42 sts x 42 rnds

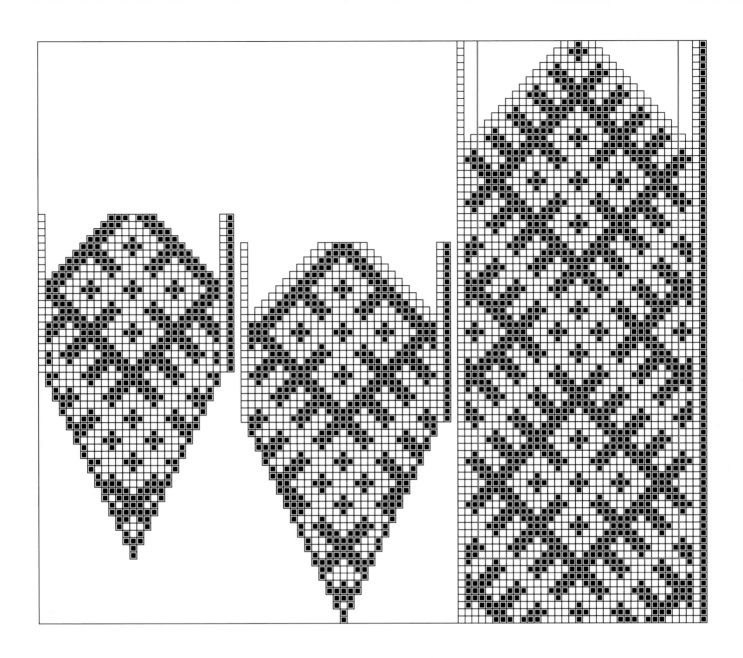

■ BURGUNDY (MC)

□ ROSE/GREY/GREEN VARIEGATED

	DK. RED (MC)
	BR. TURQUOISE
	BLUE GREEN
	LT. BLUE
	LT. GREEN

*T*he hooks off the diamonds have been connected in a zigzag pattern. It creates a very different look from the others in this pattern group, though it's somewhat similar to Mitten 25.

Size
Adult's Medium (Large)

Yarn
Nordic Fiber Arts' Rauma Finnullgarn 2-ply 100% Wool, 1¾ oz (50 g) = approx. 178 yds. (163 m) in #499 Dark Red (MC), 2 skeins; #4186 Bright Turquoise, #483 Blue Green, #451 Blue, and #4887 Green, 1 skein each.

If not available: 2-ply 100% wool, 1¾ oz (50 g) = approx. 178 yds. (163 m) in dark red (MC), 2 skeins; bright turquoise, blue green, light blue, and light green, 1 skein each.

Needles
5, size 0 U.S. (2.00 mm, 12 U.K.) double-pointed needles or size to give gauge.

Gauge
20 sts and 22 rnds = 2" (5 cm) over two-color stockinette stitch worked in the round (all k).

Cast On
80 (92) sts

Cuff
Length: 3½" (9 cm), (3¾" (9.5 cm)).
Corrugated rib knit dk. red, purl blues and greens worked in 3-rnd stripes.

Reticulation
30 sts x 30 rnds

23

Adult's Medium (Large)

Yarn

Brown Sheep Company's Nature Spun Sport weight 100% Wool, 1¾ oz. (50 g) = approx. 184 yds. (168 m) in #N 41 Turkish Olive (MC); Sport weight 100% Wool, 2 oz. (56 g) = approx. 210 yds. (192 m) in dark beige variegated, 1 skein each.

If not available: Sport weight 100% wool, 1¾ oz. (50 g) = approx. 184 yds. (168 m) in dark olive green (MC); sport-weight 100% wool, 2 oz. (56 g) = approx. 210 yds. (192 m) in dark beige variegated, 1 skein each.

Needles

5, size 2 U.S. (2.75 mm, 12 U.K.) double-pointed needles or size to give gauge.

Gauge

16 sts and 18 rnds = 2" (5 cm) over two-color stockinette stitch worked in the round (all k).

Cast On

64 (72) sts

Cuff

Length: 3½" (9 cm), (3¾" (9.5 cm)).
K2, p2 rib in dk. beige variegated.

Reticulation

30 sts x 24 rnds

*S*imilar to some of the other reticulations, this 30 sts x 24 rnds reticulation differs as its design incorporates four smaller crosses in the center of one larger diamond.

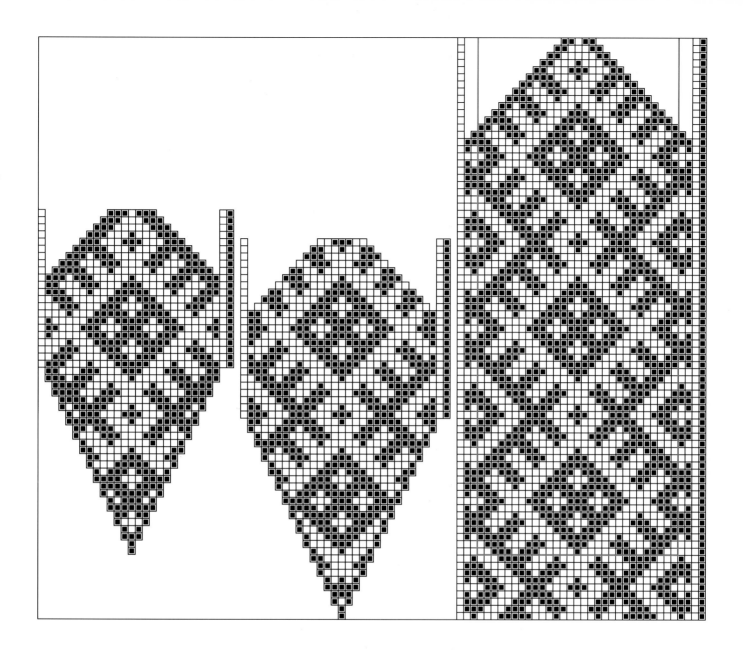

■ DK. OLIVE GREEN (MC)

☐ DK. BEIGE VARIEGATED

24

Truly a balanced design. The reticulation is dark on light at the mitten's center, while being light on dark at the sides.

Size
Adult's Medium (Large)

Yarn
Helmi Vuorelma Oy Satakieli 2-ply 100% Wool, 3½ oz. (100 g) = approx. 357 yds. (326 m) in Green (MC) and Yellow, 1 skein each.

If not available: 2-ply 100% wool, 3½ oz. (100 g) = approx. 357 yds. (326 m) in medium green (MC) and medium yellow, 1 skein each.

Needles
5, size 0 U.S. (2.00 mm, 14 U.K.) double-pointed needles or size to give gauge.

Gauge
20 sts and 22 rnds = 2" (5 cm) over two-color stockinette stitch worked in the round (all k).

Cast On
80 (92) sts

Cuff
Length: 3½" (9 cm), (3¾" (9.5 cm)).

Corrugated rib knit med. green, purl med. yellow.

Reticulation
30 sts x 24 rnds

■ MED. GREEN (MC)

☐ MED. YELLOW

The individual diagonal lines, with connecting ends, create a serpentine appearance that gives a more rounded look to the overall pattern. The reticulation is another on of the star as central motif.

Size
Adult's Medium (Large)

Yarn
Brown Sheep Company's Nature Spun Fingering weight 100% Wool, 1¾ oz. (50 g) = approx. 310 yds. (283 m) in #N 72 Metropolis Turquoise (MC), #N 78 Turquoise Wonder (MC), #N 77 Azure (MC), #750 White Port, #308 Sunburst Gold, #N 15 Gold Glow, and #N 13 Bluff Brown, 1 skein each.

If not available: Fingering weight 100% wool, 1¾ oz. (50 g) = approx. 310 yds. (283 m) in dark turquoise (MC), medium turquoise (MC), light turquoise (MC), off-white, medium gold, light gold, and gold brown, 1 skein each.

Needles
5, size 1 U.S. (2.25 mm, 13 U.K.) double-pointed needles or size to give gauge.

Gauge
20 sts and 22 rnds = 2" (5 cm) over two-color stockinette stitch worked in the round (all k).

Cast On
80 (92) sts

Cuff
Length: 3½" (9 cm) (3¾" 9.5 cm)).
Corrugated rib knit dk. turquoise, purl in gold colors, shading in stripes from gold brown to off-white then back to gold brown.

Reticulation
36 sts x 48 rnds

■ TURQUOISES (MC)

☐ OFF–WHITE AND GOLDS

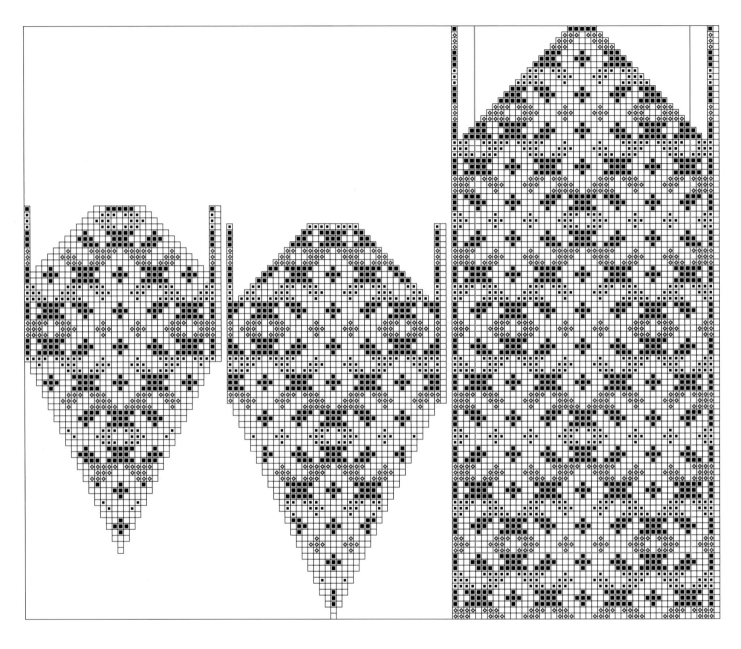

	BROWN HEATHER (MC)
■	PALE TURQUOISE
■	LT. TURQUOISE,
◇	LT. GREY GREEN

This motif is related to mitten 13.

Size
Adult's Medium (Large)

Yarn
Brown Sheep Company's Nature Spun Fingering weight 100% Wool 1¾ oz. (50 g) = approx. 310 yds. (283 m) in #701 Stone (MC), #N 53 Arctic Turquoise, #N 76 Antique Turquoise, and #N 20 Arctic Moss, 1 skein each.

If not available: Fingering-weight 100% wool 1¾ oz. (50 g) = approx. 310 yds. (283 m) in brown heather (MC), pale turquoise, light turquoise, light grey green, 1 skein each.

Needles
5, size 1 U.S. (2.25 mm, 13 U.K.) double-pointed needles or size to give gauge.

Gauge
20 sts and 22 rnds = 2" (5 cm) over two-color stockinette stitch worked in the round (all k).

Cast On
80 (92)

Cuff
Length: 3½" (9 cm), (3¾" (9.5 cm)).

Corrugated rib knit brown heather, purl turquoises and grey green.

Reticulation
24 sts x 36 rnds

27

Reminiscent of Scandinavian knitting, this simple reticulation is highlighted by a 2 sts x 2 rnds checkerboard for the thumb and tip.

Size
Adult's Medium (Large)

Yarn
Brown Sheep Company's Nature Spun Sport weight 100% Wool, 1¾ oz. (50 g) = approx. 184 yds. (268 m) in #N 03 Grey Heather and #N 41 Turkish Olive (MC), 1 skein each.

If not available: Sport weight 100% Wool, 1¾ oz. (50 g) = approx. 184 yds. (268 m) in light heather grey and medium olive green (MC), 1 skein each.

Needles
5, size 2 U.S. (2.75 mm, 12 U.K.) double-pointed needles or size to give gauge.

Gauge
16 sts and 18 rnds = 2" (5 cm) over two-color stockinette stitch worked in the round (all k).

Cast On
80 (92) sts

Cuff
Length: 3½" (9 cm), 3¾" (9.5 cm)).
Corrugated rib knit med. heather grey, purl med. olive green.

Reticulation
6 sts x 8 rnds

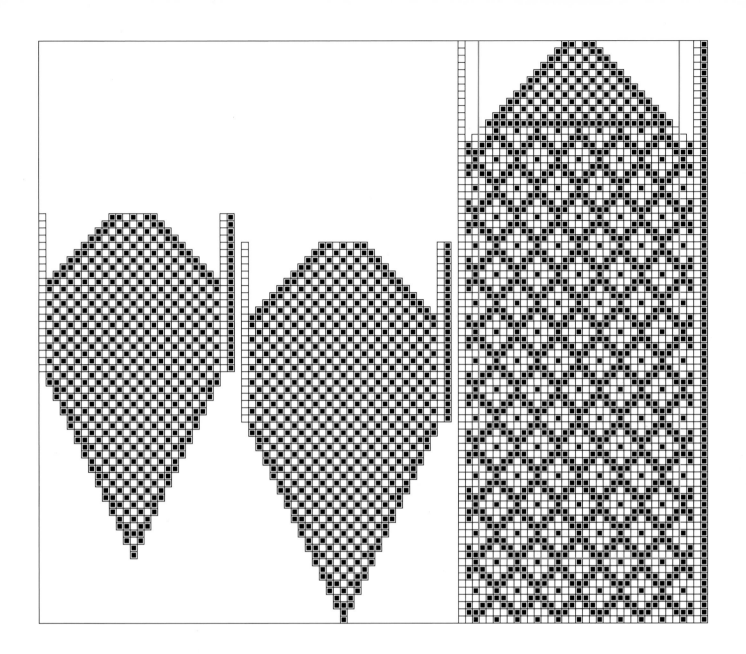

LT. HEATHER GREY

■ MED. OLIVE GREEN (MC)

28

As you can see, the pattern looks quite different when worked light on dark than it does worked dark on light. The pattern is unusual in that it combines two elements that are not commonly used, the diamond with nine crosses and a cross placed at the center of another.

Size
Adult's Medium (Large)

Yarn
Brown Sheep Company's Nature Spun Fingering weight 100% Wool, 1¾ Oz. (50 g) = approx. 310 yds. (283 m) in #601 Pepper, 1 skein; Fingering weight 100% wool, 1¾ oz. (50 g) = approx. 310 yds. (283 m) in red/gold/orange variegated, 1 skein.

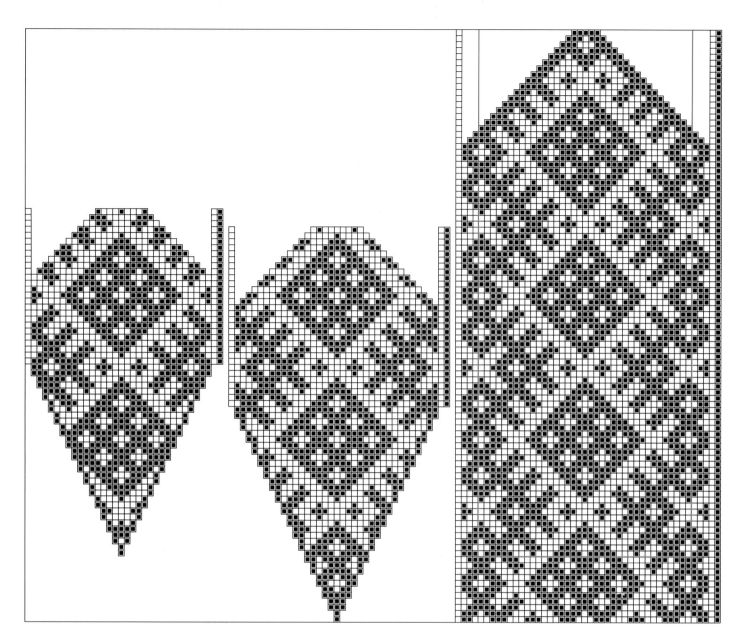

If not available: Fingering weight 100% wool, 1¾ Oz. (50 g) = approx. 310 yds. (283 m) in black (MC) and red/gold/orange variegated, 1 skein each.

Needles

5, size 1 U.S. (2.25 mm, 13 U.K.) double-pointed needles or size to give gauge.

Gauge

20 sts and 22 rnds = 2" (5 cm) over two-color stockinette stitch worked in the round (all k).

Cast On

80 (92) sts

Cuff

Length: 3½" (9 cm), (3¾" (9.5 cm)).

Corrugated rib knit black, purl variegated red/gold/orange.

Reticulation

36 sts x 24 rnds

■ BLACK (MC)

□ RED/GOLD/ORANGE VARIEGATED

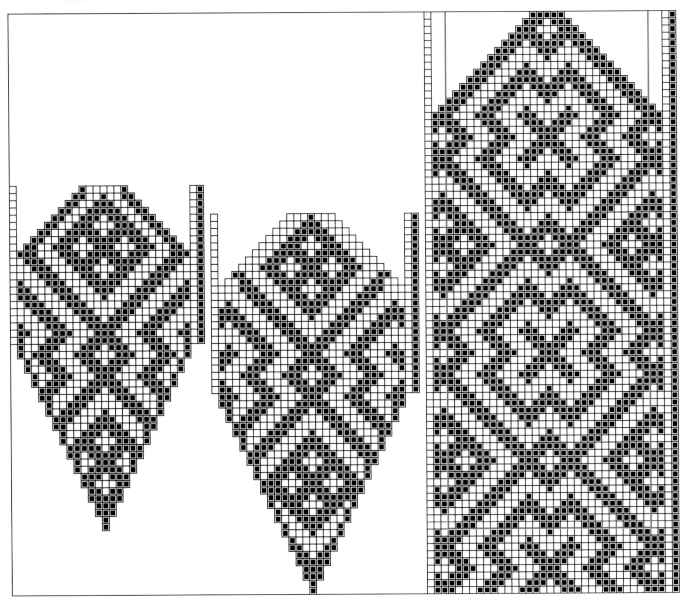

29

■ VARIEGATED BURGUNDY (MC)

□ DUSTY PINK

I designed this reticulation following a combination of rules for patterning. By starting with a four-row-wide border with a 30-stitch repeat, I was able to create this interesting design.

Size
Adult's Medium (Large)

Yarn
Brown Sheep Company's Nature Spun Sport weight 100% Wool, 1¾ oz (50 g) = approx. 184 yds. (168 m) in #N 87 Victorian Pink, 1 skein; Sport weight 100% wool, 2 oz. (56 g) = approx. 210 yds.(192 m) in variegated burgundy, 1 skein.

If not available: Sport weight 100% wool, 1¾ oz (50 g) = approx. 184 yds. (168 m) in dusty pink, 1 skein; sport weight 100% wool, 2 oz. (56 g) = approx. 210 yds.(192 m) in variegated burgundy (MC), 1 skein.

Needles
5, size 2 U.S.(2.75 mm, 12 U.K.) double-pointed needles or size to give gauge.

Gauge
16 sts and 18 rnds = 2" (5 cm) over two-color stockinette stitch worked in the round (all k).

Cast On
64 (72) sts

Cuff
Length: 3½"(9 cm), 3¾"(9.5cm)).

Corrugated rib knit variegated burgundy, purl dusty rose.

Reticulation
30 sts x 30 rnds

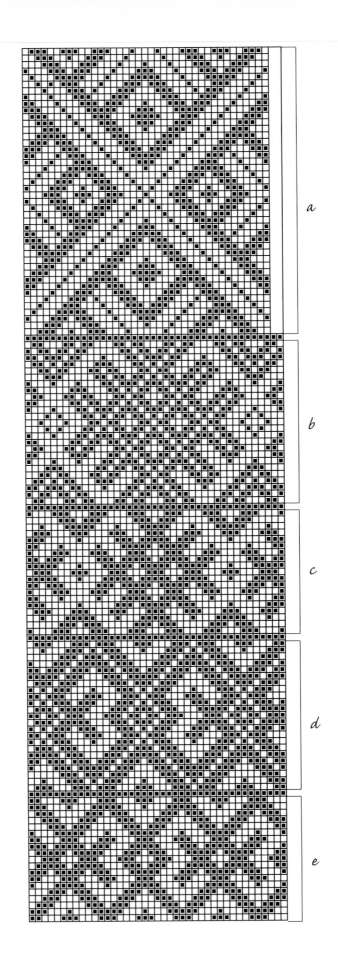

Complex Borders and Complex Reticulations

These patterns seem to have been developed later by more skillful knitters who could either remember more complicated patterns or use pencil and paper for charting. They are expansions of the 3 x 3 reticulation into a 2,1,2, 3,1,3 or 2,1,1,1,2.

In the chart showing the examples of the patterns (a), from Mitten 35, varies more than the those used for borders such as (b) from Mitten 32, (d) showing one horizontal repeat of the pattern in Mitten 34, and (e) showing the border used in Mitten 14.

30

■ DK. GREEN (MC)

· DUSTY ROSE

☐ GOLD

*T*his mitten is designed with sophisticated Komi patterns; the main border and the x-style septenary border at the wrist. The hand portion of the mitten has two patterns, each with four-stitch repeats.

Size
Adult's Medium (Large)

Yarn
Nordic Fiber Arts' Rauma Finnullgarn 2-ply 100% Wool, 1¾ oz. (50 g) = approx. 178 yds. (163 m) in #485 Dark Green (MC), 2 skeins; #490 Rose and #492 Gold, 1 skein each.

If not available: 2-ply 100% wool, 1¾ oz. (50 g) = approx. 178 yds. (163 m) in dark green (MC), 2 skeins; dusty rose and gold, 1 skein each.

Needles
5, size 3 U.S. (3.25 mm, 10 U.K.) double-pointed needles or size to give gauge.

Gauge
16 sts and 18 rnds = 2" (5 cm) over two-color stockinette stitch worked in the round (all k).

Cast On
64 (72) sts

Cuff
Length: 3½" (9 cm), (3¾" (9.5 cm)).
Corrugated rib knit dk. green, purl gold and dusty rose worked in alternate 7-rnd stripes.

Reticulation
24 rnd-wide main border

31

The border is a version of a star pattern (commonly found in Scandinavian knitting) which is said to have been brought to the Komi from Russian women who immigrated to the area. The design also includes a septenary border, a simple reticulation over the fingers, and a four-stitch repeat at the wrist.

Size
Adult Medium (Large)

Yarn
Brown Sheep Company's Nature Spun Fingering weight 100% Wool, 1¾ oz. (50 g) = approx. 310 yds.(283 m)) in #N 03 Grey Heather, #730 Natural, #N 46 Fox Red (MC), #880 Charcoal (MC), and #601 Pepper (MC), 1 skein each.

If not available: Fingering weight 100% wool, 1¾ oz. (50 g) = approx. 310 yds.(283 m) in light heather grey, white, red (MC), dark grey (MC), and black (MC), 1 skein each.

Needles
5, size 1 U.S. (2.25 mm, 13 U.K.) double-pointed needles or size to give gauge.

Gauge
20 sts and 22 rnds = 2" (5 cm) over two-color stockinette stitch worked in the round (all k).

Cast On
80 (92) sts

Cuff
Length: 3½" (9 cm), (3¾" (9.5 cm)).
Corrugated rib knit dk. grey, purl lt. heather grey.

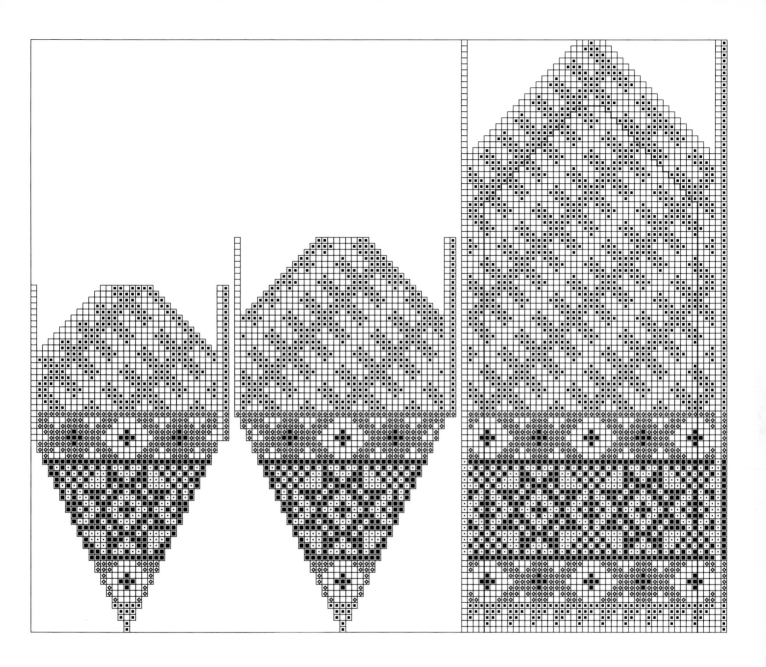

<table>
<tr><td>☐</td><td>LT. HEATHER GREY</td></tr>
<tr><td>·</td><td>WHITE</td></tr>
<tr><td>■</td><td>RED (MC)</td></tr>
<tr><td>▪</td><td>DK. GREY (MC)</td></tr>
<tr><td>◇</td><td>BLACK (MC)</td></tr>
</table>

32

☐ LT. HEATHER GREY (MC)

■ MED. DUSTY ROSE

▪ MED. TURQUOISE

*T*he wide border in this design is an expansion of the popular three-line cross. It also uses a stacked four-stitch pattern of diagonal lines with a zigzag.

Size
Adult's Medium (Large)

Yarn
Brown Sheep Company's Nature Spun Fingering weight 100% Wool, 1¾" (50 g) = approx. 310 yds. (283 m) in #N 03 Grey Heather (MC), #N 99 Pagan Pink, and #N 72 Metropolis Turquoise, 1 skein each.

If not available: Fingering-weight 100% wool, 1¾" (50 g) = approx. 310 yds. (283 m) in light heather grey (MC), medium dusty rose, and medium turquoise, 1 skein each.

Needles
5, size 1 U.S. (2.25 mm, 13 U.K.) double-pointed needles or size to give gauge.

Gauge
20 sts and 22 rnds = 2" (5 cm) over two-color stockinette stitch worked in the round (all k).

Cast On
80 (92) sts

Cuff
Length: 3½" (9 cm), (3¾" (9.5 cm)).

Corrugated rib knit lt. heather grey, purl med. dusty rose.

Reticulation
32 sts x 32 rnds

33

With one complex border and a 10-round border related to the three-line cross, this mitten uses a very popular pattern for combining borders and reticulations.

Size
Adult's Medium (Large)

Yarn
Brown Sheep Company's Nature Spun Fingering weight 100% Wool, 1¾ oz. (50 g) = approx. 310 yds. (283 m) in #N 15 Gold Glow, #N 65 Sapphire (MC), and #N 56 Meadow Green (MC), 1 skein each.

If not available: Fingering weight 100% wool, 1¾ oz. (50 g) = approx. 310 yds. (283 m) in gold, medium purple (MC), and light green (MC), 1 skein each.

Needles
5, size 1 U.S. (2.25 mm, 13 U.K.) double-pointed needles or size to give gauge.

Gauge
20 sts and 22 rnds = 2" (5 cm) over two-color stockinette stitch worked in the round (all k).

Cast On
80 (92) sts

Cuff
Length: 3½" (9 cm), (3¾" (9.5 cm)).
Corrugated rib knit gold, purl lt. green and med. purple worked in alternating stripes.

GOLD

MED. PURPLE (MC)

LT. GREEN (MC)

34

If this pattern looks familiar, it's because it's an expansion of the wide-border belt pattern from Mitten 14. Also included in this design are a four-stitch diagonal and a four-round border.

Size
Adult's Medium (Large)

Yarn
Brown Sheep Company's Nature Spun Fingering weight 100% Wool, 1¾ oz. (50 g) = approx. 310 yds. (283 m) in #N 03 Grey Heather, #N 30 Nordic Blue, #110 Blueberry, and #N 48 Scarlet, 1 skein each.

If not available: Fingering weight 100% wool, 1¾ oz. (50 g) = approx. 310 yds. (283 m) in light heather grey, medium blue (MC), dark blue (MC), and dark red, 1 skein each.

Needles
5, size 1 U.S. (2.25 mm, 13 U.K.) double-pointed needles or size to give gauge.

Gauge
20 sts and 22 rnds = 2" (5 cm) over two-color stockinette stitch worked in the round (all k).

Cast On
80 (92) sts

Cuff
Length: 3½ (9 cm), (3¾" (9.5 cm)).

Corrugated rib knit lt. heather grey, purl med. blue.

Reticulation
32 sts x 28 rnds

☐ LT. HEATHER GREY

■ MED. BLUE (MC),

◇ DK. BLUE (MC)

· DK. RED

35

- ■ NAVY (MC)
- + LT. GREEN
- ◇ BLUE GREEN
- ⊠ MED. BLUE
- · LAVENDER
- ☐ MED. PINK

*T*he asymmetrical nature
of the diamond and the
reticulation with one pattern
repeated over both axes, makes
this a very interesting patten.

Size
Adult's Medium (Large)

Yarn
Nordic Fiber Arts' Rauma Finnullgarn
2-ply 100% Wool, 1¾ oz. (50 g) =
approx. 178 yds. (163 m) in #459 Navy
(MC), 2 skeins; #4887 Green, #483
Teal, #451 Blue, #473 Lavender, and
#4571 Pink, 1 skein each.

If not available: 2-ply 100% wool, 1¾
oz. (50 g) = approx. 178 yds. (163 m)
navy blue (MC), 2 skeins; light green,
blue green, medium blue, lavender, and
medium pink,, 1 skein each.

Needles
5, size 0 U.S. (2 mm, 14 U.K.) double-
pointed needles or size to give gauge.

Gauge
20 sts and 22 rounds = 2" (5 cm) over
two-color stockinette stitch worked in
the round (all k).

Cast On
80 (92) sts

Cuff
Length: 3½"(9 cm), (3¾" (9.5 cm)).
Corrugated rib knit navy, purl progression
of colors worked in stripes starting with
green to pink and back to green.

Reticulation
44 sts x 44 rnds

36

A recent traveler to the Komi Republic showed me a pair of contemporary-knit mittens. This pattern is copied from that design.

Size
Adult's Medium (Large)

Yarn
Nordic Fiber Arts' Rauma Finnullgarn 2-ply 100% Wool, 1¾ oz. (50 g) = approx. 178 yds. (163 m)) in #474 Purple (MC), 2 skeins; #4088 Lavender and #450 Gold, 1 skein each.

If not available: 2-ply 100% wool, 1¾ oz. (50 g) = approx. 178 yds. (163 m)) in purple (MC), 2 skeins; lavender and gold, 1 skein each.

Needles
5, size 3 U.S. (3.25 mm, 10 U.K.) double-pointed needles or size to give gauge.

Gauge
16 sts and 18 rnds = 2" (5 cm) over two-color stockinette stitch worked in the round (all k).

Cast On
64 (72) sts

Cuff
Length: 3½" (9 cm), (3¾" (9.5 cm)).

K2, p2 rib worked in stripes, 16 (18) rnds purple, 2 rnds lavender, 4 rnds purple, 3 rnds gold, 4 rnds purple, 2 rnds lavender, 16 (18) rnds purple.

Reticulation
28 sts X 28 rnds

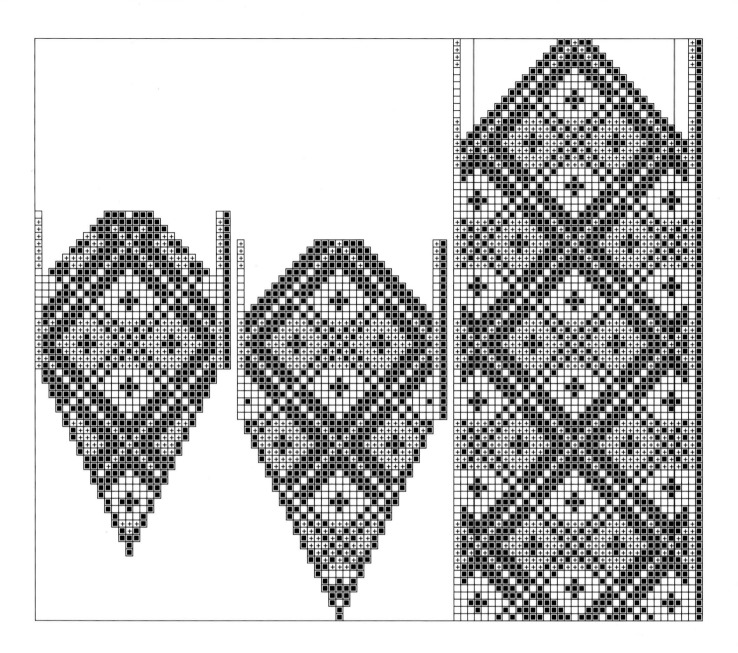

■   PURPLE (MC)

☐   LAVENDER

+   GOLD

Komi Fez with Tassels

*T*his cap matches Mitten 16 on page 58.

Sizes

Child's Medium (Large); Adult's Medium (Large). Finished measurements 16"(40.5 cm), (18"(45.5 cm), 20"(51 cm), 22"(56 cm)).

Yarn

Nordic Fiber Arts' Rauma Finnullgarn 2-ply 100% wool, 1¾ oz. (50 g) = approx. 178 yds. (163 m) in #446 Blue, skeins; #401 White, #415 Red, and #450 Gold, 1 skein each.

If not available: 2-ply 100% wool, 1¾ oz. (50 g) = approx. 178 yds. (163 m) in blue, white, red, and gold, 1 skein each.

Needles

1, 16" (40.5 cm) circular needle, size 3 U.S.(3.25 mm, 10 U.K.) or size needed to give gauge.

Gauge

16 sts and 18 rnds = 2" (5 cm) over two-color st st worked in the round (all K).

Instructions

Cast 126 (144); 162 (180) sts on circular needle. Join, being careful not to twist. Begin k1, p1 rib; insert marker at the end of 1st rnd. Continue in k1, p1 rib for 1" (2.5 cm). Follow chart, working until you have 6" (15 cm), 7" (12.5 cm); 8" (20 cm), 9" (22.5 cm) above the cast on.

Bind off loosely. Turn cap inside out to sew 3 points together. With a tapestry needle and piece of yarn about 24" (61 cm) long, move 21 (24); 27 (30) sts from

the end of cast off. Begin by sewing the 21st and 22nd sts (24 & 25); 27 & 28 (30 & 31) together, working until you get back to beg of rnd. You now have ⅓ of the cap sewn together (one point of three). Take the middle stitch of what is unsewn, and bring it beside the needle and yarn. Work the 2nd point as the 1st. Break off the yarn. Return to the center and sew the 3rd point. Weave in all the ends.

To make a tassel, wind yarn around a 4" (10 cm) wide piece of cardboard 40 times. Cut 6 strands of yarn 24" (61 cm) long. Place the strands through the yarn wound on the cardboard. Pull so the ends are even, then braid 3 sections of 4 strands each, (making a braid approx. 5" (12.5 cm) long. Tie a knot in the end of the braid. Secure the end of the tassel about 1"(2.5 cm) from where the braid is attached by taking a piece of yarn and winding it around the tassel 3 times tightly. Make two more tassels. Cut the ends of the tassels. Attach the knotted end of each braid to each corner of the top of the cap.

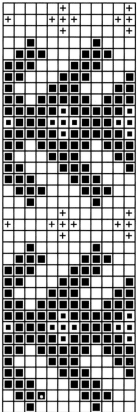

■ BLUE

□ WHITE

+ RED

■ GOLD

Komi Cap

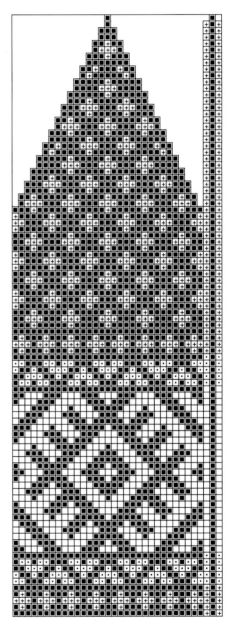

Size

Adult's Medium. Finished cap measures 20" (51 cm).

Yarn

School House Press' Satakieli Sport weight Yarn 100% wool, 3½ oz (100 g) = approx. 360 yds. (329 m) in 1½ oz (50 g) Green, 1 oz. (25 g) Yellow, ½ oz. (10 g) Orange, 1 oz. (25 g) Red.

If not available: Sport weight yarn 100% wool, 3½ oz (100 g) = approx. 360 yds. (329 m) in 1½ oz (50 g) green, 1 oz. (25 g) yellow, ½ oz. (10 g) orange, 1 oz. (25 g) red.

Needles

1, 16" (40.5 cm) circular needle, size 0 U.S. (2 mm, 14 U.K.) or size needed to give gauge. 5, size 0 U.S. (2 mm, 14 U.K.) dpn.

Gauge

10 sts and 11 rnds = 1" (2.5 cm).

Instructions

Begin with cuff. Cast 204 sts in green on circular needle, join, being careful not to twist. Work k2, p2 ribbing for 1" (2.5 cm). After the 1st rnd of ribbing, place a marker on the needle.

When you complete the ribbing, begin working pattern from the bottom right-hand corner of the chart. There are 6 repeats of the pattern around the cap.

Decrease for the crown, beginning on rnd 65. Work the dec as follows: work the first 3 seam stitches, ssk, k to within 2 sts of the next seam line, k2tog, continue to work the chart around. Work the next round without dec.

On round 93, work the 3 seam sts, then work a double dec with the last 3 sts of the repeat as follows: sl1, k2tog, psso. When working the final rnd, work with MC only and work the double dec as on round 93, k1, work around. There should be 12 sts left.

Break off a tail of about 12" (30.5 cm). Thread a tapestry needle and draw the end through the remaining stitches, pulling it snug, and weaving into the inside of cap. Weave in all the ends.

■	GREEN
□	YELLOW
·	ORANGE
+	RED

Sock with Peasant Heel

Size
Ladies' Small

Yarn
Renaissance Yarns' Froehlich-Wolle Special Blauband 80% Wool, 20% Nylon, 1¾ oz. (50g) = approx. 225 yards (206 m) in #1 grey, #55 teal, 2 skeins each.

If not available: sock yarn, 80% wool, 20% nylon, 1¾ oz. (50g) = approx. 225 yards (206 m) in grey and blue green, 2 skeins each.

Waste yarn
1 yd. (.92 m).

Needles
5, size 0 U.S. (2 mm, 14 U.K.) dpn or size to give gauge.

Gauge
11 sts and 12 rnds = 1"(2.5 cm).

Instructions
CO 88 sts blue green using long-tail method. Divide the sts onto 4 needles (24 on 1st and 3rd needle and 20 on 2nd and 4th). Join, being careful not to twist. Work 1" (2.5 cm) of k2, p2 ribbing. Work two complete (or the number length of sock you wish) repeats of the leg chart, then knit 21 more rounds. Begin heel preparation on round 22.

Begin heel preparation. knit first 2 sts of the rnd (one blue green, one grey). With waste yarn, k41 sts. Break off waste yarn. Slide the sts back to the beg of the rnd (where the waste yarn begins—don't

reknit the 2 seam stitches). Continue knitting the rnd with the full pattern. Continue the 3rd repeat of the reticulation, then knit 2 more repeats for the foot. Work 11 rnds of the toe chart, then begin shaping toe which is 1¾" (4.5 cm) long. If you need a longer sock, continue knitting the pattern and rechart toe, or knit toe in a solid color.

Dec the toe according to chart as follows: 1st needle: k2 from chart (One MC, one CC) ssk in pattern color, k to eon; 2nd needle: knit to within 3 stitches of the eon, k2tog in pattern, k1; 3rd needle: as 1st needle; 4th needle: as 2nd needle.

Continue working the chart until there are 16 sts on all the needles, 4 on each. Transfer the sts on 2nd needle to 1st needle, and the sts on 4th needle, to 3rd needle.

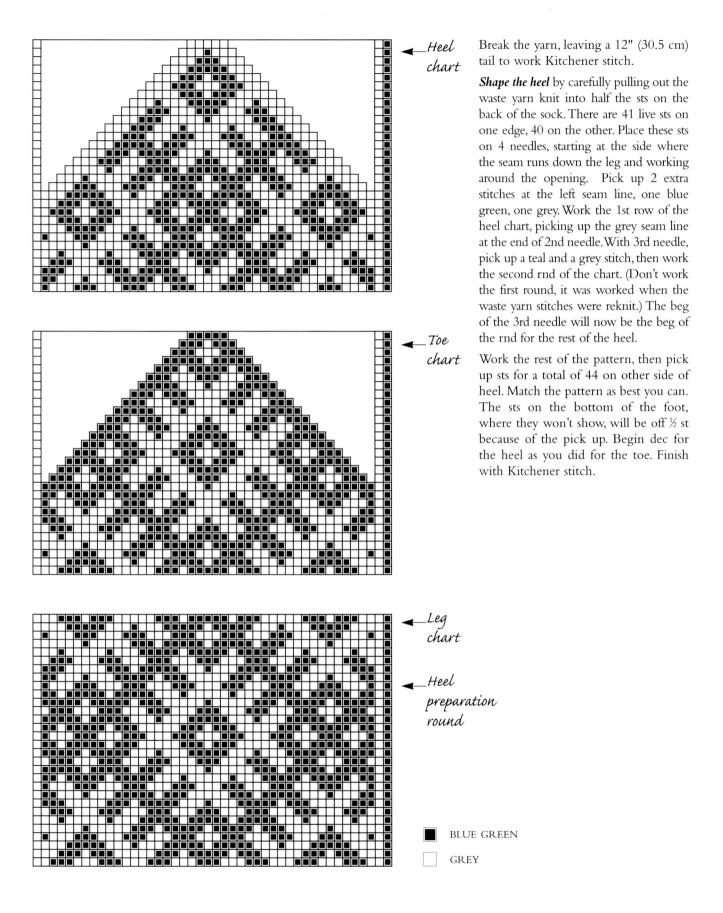

← Heel chart

← Toe chart

← Leg chart

← Heel preparation round

Break the yarn, leaving a 12" (30.5 cm) tail to work Kitchener stitch.

Shape the heel by carefully pulling out the waste yarn knit into half the sts on the back of the sock. There are 41 live sts on one edge, 40 on the other. Place these sts on 4 needles, starting at the side where the seam runs down the leg and working around the opening. Pick up 2 extra stitches at the left seam line, one blue green, one grey. Work the 1st row of the heel chart, picking up the grey seam line at the end of 2nd needle. With 3rd needle, pick up a teal and a grey stitch, then work the second rnd of the chart. (Don't work the first round, it was worked when the waste yarn stitches were reknit.) The beg of the 3rd needle will now be the beg of the rnd for the rest of the heel.

Work the rest of the pattern, then pick up sts for a total of 44 on other side of heel. Match the pattern as best you can. The sts on the bottom of the foot, where they won't show, will be off ½ st because of the pick up. Begin dec for the heel as you did for the toe. Finish with Kitchener stitch.

■ BLUE GREEN

□ GREY

Sock with Shaped Heel

Size

Mens' Medium

Yarn

Knitting Traditions' Creskeld Guernsey Wool 5-ply 100% wool, 3½ oz. (100 g) = approx. 246 yds. (225 m) in red and black, 2 skeins each.

If not available: 5-ply 100% wool, 3½ oz. (100 g) = approx. 246 yds. (225 m) in red and black, 2 skeins each.

Needles

5, size 2 U.S. (2.75 mm, 12 U.K.) 8" (20.5 cm) dpn or size to give gauge. Blunt-pointed wool needle

Gauge

8 sts and 9 rows = 1" (2.5 cm).

Instructions

CO loosely 84 sts. Divide sts evenly on 3 or 4 needles (working the initial ribbing is more stable over 3 needles). Join into a round, being careful not to twist sts. This join marks the seam line and beg of the rnd. Work k2, p2 rib for 2" (5 cm). For leg, work the chart establishing seam stitches on sides (beg of rnd will be at the left seam line, not at center back)

Work heel flap and turned heel in black only. Add reinforcing yarn if desired, k41 sts. Turn work, sl1, p40 sts. Place remaining 43 sts onto one needle to hold for instep. Work back and forth on the heel sts only, starting with the right side facing, ★sl1, k1, repeat from ★ across row. Next row, sl1, p to end of row. Repeat these 2 rows 18 times more. You will have a total of 40 heel rows and 21 chain-edge stitches. End ready to start a right-side row.

Turn the heel with round-heel shaping made with a series of short rows. k22, sl1, k1, psso, k1, turn work. Next row, sl1, p5, p2tog, p 1, turn. Next row, sl1, k to within 1 st away from gap, sl1, k1, psso, k1, turn. Next row, sl1, p to within 1 st away from gap, p2tog, p1, turn. Continue, always working the 2 sts on each side of the gap together. When all sts are gone from both sides, k to the middle of the right-side row, break off reinforcing thread.

Beg heel gusset by k the 2nd half of heel sts onto the needle with the 1st half of the heel stitches. With the same needle, pick up and k20 sts along the right side of the heel. With the empty needle, work pattern across instep. With the remaining empty needle, pick up and k20 sts in red and black from the chart along the left side heel. Work across the remaining heel sts in pattern. While working the leg of the sock, the beg of the rnd was on the left side of the sock.

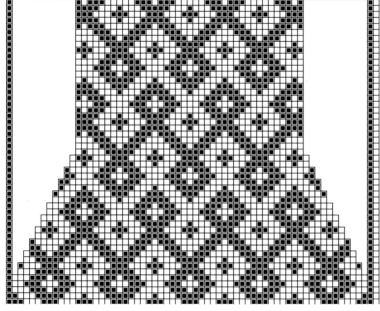

After working the heel the beg of the rnd is now on the right side of the sock.

You should have ½ the instep sts on 1st needle, ½ the instep sts on 2nd, left-side gusset sts plus ½ the heel sts on 3rd needle, and right-side gusset sts plus ½ the heel sts on 4th needle. If not, adjust sts accordingly. The rnd beg on the right side of the sock.

Shape the gusset beg on the next rnd by working the instep sts on 1st and 2nd needles, then on 3rd needle k2, ssk, k to eon, k to 3 sts away from the end of 4th needle, k2tog, k1. On next rnd, work in pattern stitch without dec. Repeat these 2 rounds, dec at the beg. of 2nd needle and end 3rd needle until you have a total of 84 sts with 21 sts on each needle. Cont in pattern until the foot measures 3" (7.5 cm) less than desired length from heel to toe. If you need to change the length, re-chart the toe or knit it in a solid color.

Shape the toe beg on next rnd by first adding reinforcing thread if desired, then 1st needle, k2 from chart, ssk, k to eon. Work to 3 sts away from end of 2nd needle, k2tog, k1. K1, ssk at beg. of 3rd needle, work to 3 sts away from end of 4th needle, k2tog, k1. Next rnd, work st st in pattern until there are a total of 16 sts, 4 on each needle. Distribute 8 sts on each of two needles. Cut yarn, leaving a 12" (30.5 cm) tail to work Kitchener stitch.

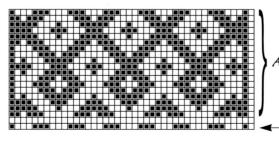

} *A*

← *Work this round once, then work A, the 18-rnd repeat.*

■ BLACK

□ RED

Alternative Ways of Working the Mittens

Using Circular Needles

Some people have trouble managing double-pointed needles or have stitches fall off when working with them. This may be a solution to your difficulties.

With two 16" (40.5 cm) dp circular needles, arrange the stitches for the palm on one (needle #1) and the stitches for the back on the other (needle #2). Using only needle #1, work in a circle around the palm and half of the thumb stitches. When you get to the middle of the thumb, drop needle #1, pick up needle #2 and work in a circle across the second half of the thumb stitches and then the back of the mitten. Note: The stitches on each needle do not make a circle, the stitches on both needles make the circle. Continue working around in this manner.

Knitting Flat and Sewing the Seam

Inc 1 st when casting on to make a seam stitch: children's mittens will be 49 (57); adult's gauge 8, 65 (73); and adult's gauge 10, 81 (93). In knitting the cuff pattern, duplicate the first and end sts: if you're working k2, p2 ribbing the first 2 sts will be a k2 and the end of the row will be k2, pP k2, k1. The first and last k sts will each provide ½ st for the seam which will be invisible. When picking up sts for the thumb, add one st for the seam at the inside of the thumb. Or, work the thumb in the rnd with dpn if you prefer.

Machine Knitting Instructions

For machine knitting, work the mitten beginning on the thumb-side of the hand (see chart). Note that the chart is an example for Mitten 15. You will need to adjust the other mitten charts accordingly.

Cast on the indicated number of sts plus one (for seam stitch). Work the cuff as indicated (the first and last sts of the row will be the same and ½ of each will be used as the seam). This is easier for a patterned cuff since you work in st st; with a ribbed cuff one side will be k2, p2, and the other side will be k2, p2, k1.

Shape the thumb gusset with full-fashioned inc, every other row as follows: Move the first st at each side out by 1 needle. Pick up the purl bar to make a st on the empty needle. Knit 2 rows in pattern. Move the first 2 sts on each side out by 1 needle, pick up the purl bar. Move the first 3 sts at each side

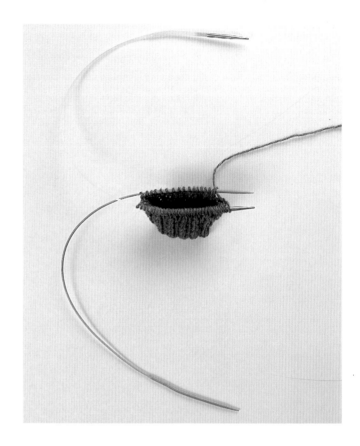

out by 1 needle. Continue in this manner until all the increases have been made at each side. After the last inc, k1 row.

Set carriage to hold needles in holding position. Hold thumb sts on side opposite carriage and k1 row. Note row count. If you have a punch card or electronic patterning machine, you will need to turn of the pattern or hold the card when scrapping off. Hold hand stitches. Remove working colors from carriage and scrap off thumb sts still in work position. Then scrap off other thumb sts.

Return row counter to row-counter setting before you scrap off the thumbs. Make 1 st at each edge by picking up the purl bar of edge stitch and hanging it on the empty needle. Continue to k until the dec for the top of the hand. Note row counter. Hold half the hand sts (include center seam st in first half worked). Work tip of mitten and place last 9 sts on holder. Reset row counter, inc 1 st at center of mitten to make the other half of the seam stitch. Work the second mitten tip, placing 9 sts on a holder.

Turn side edges of mitten towards each other as if to seam. Fold back waste and with wrong side facing you, rehang all thumb sts on machine with side edges at the center and doubling center sts. Make 1 st at each outer edge. K1 row, make 1 st each at the outer edge. K the thumb sts and decrease according to the chart.

To finish, use yarn tails to work Kitchener stitch at the top of the mitten and thumb. Use tails to sew seams in cuff, side of hand, and thumb.

Add another stitch when working second top.

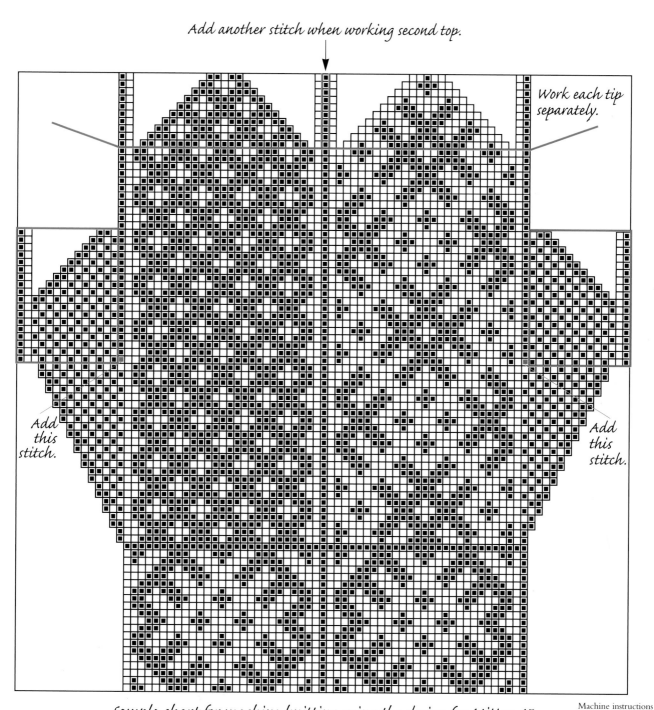

Work each tip separately.

Add this stitch.

Add this stitch.

Sample chart for machine knitting using the design for Mitten 15.

Machine instructions by Susan Guagliumi

Acknowledgements

To Anne Tompkins, my mother, who patiently taught me to knit (multiple times), who gave me an appreciation for things Eastern European, and who test knitted some very early instructions. To Susan Guagliumi, for her encouragement, support, and belief that there really was a book. To Sergei Bunaev and Mark Havill, for sensitive translation. To Al Bersbach for his generosity in sharing his adventure in the Komi Republic on his web site, and for lending me his Komi mittens and socks. To Val Gates, for his time on the phone and the loan of socks and mittens. To Debbie Grimletz, Beth Brown-Reinsel, and Meg Swansen, for yarn patience and encouragement. To Debbie MacInerny, for her help with color selection during the home stretch. To Liz Clouthier, for her thoughtful comments on the mitten pattern and test-knitting help, and to the rest of the knitters of the Nutmeg Knitters and Nutmeg Spinning Guild, especially Ellen Rozden, Selma Miriam, and Irene Kubilius. To Sue Wallace, for her words of wisdom about mittens and the resource of her knitting library. To those at Lark Books who pulled all this together, especially Rob Pulleyn, who had the vision that made this real, allowing the knitting world to see and disseminate these patterns. And finally to Jane LaFerla, my editor, for her work, patience, and diplomacy.

SOURCES

Brown Sheep Nature Spun, Sports-Weight and Fingering-Weight, and Creskeld Guernsey Yarn
Knitting Traditions
PO Box 421
Delta, PA 17314
(717) 456-7950
(Beth Brown-Reinsel)

Dale Helio
Patternworks
PO Box 1690
Poughkeepsie, NY 12601
(800) 438-5464

Have You Any Wool?
Cheshire, CT 06410
(203) 699-9633
(Susan Guagliumi)

Helmi Vuorelma Oy Satakieli Finnish Yarn
Schoolhouse Press
6899 Cary Bluff
Pittsville, WI 54466
(715) 884-2799
(Meg Swansen)

Rauma Finullgarn Yarn
Nordic Fiber Arts
4 Cutts Road
Durham, NH 03824
(603) 868-1196

CANADA

Brown Sheep Yarns in Canada:
Hill Knittery
10720 Yonge
Richmond Hill, Ontario L4C3C9
Canada
(905) 770-4341

BIBLIOGRAPHY

Gottfridsson, Inger and Gottfridsson Ingrid, *The Mitten Book.* Asheville, NC: Lark Books, 1985.

Hansen, Robin, with Janetta Dexter. *Flying Geese & Partridge Feet: More Mittens from Up North and Down East.* Camden, ME: Down East, 1986.

Hansen, Robin. *Fox & Geese & Fences: A Collection of Traditional Maine Mittens.* Camden, ME: Down East, 1983.

Harlow, Eve (Ed), *The Art of Knitting.* London & Glasgow: William Collins and Sons, 1977.

Kalashnikova, NM. *National Costumes of the Soviet People.* Moscow: Planeta, 1990.

Klimnova, Galina Nikolaevna, *Uzornoe Viazanie Komi (Knitted Patterns of the Komi).* Syktvkar, Komi Republic, Russia: Komi Book Publishing House, 1978.

Sawnsen, Meg. *Wool Gathering #55.* Wisconsin, 1996.

Upitis, Lizbeth. *Latvian Mittens: Traditional Designs & Techniques.* St. Paul, MN: DosTejedoras, 1981.

INDEX

We'd like to hear from you . . . .

Let us know what you think of your new Lark Book. We want to produce the best, most useful and good-looking craft books possible, and your comments will help us do that. We'd also like to send you a free copy of our most recent catalog.

Mostly Mittens

Comments: . . . .

. . . .

. . . .

. . . .

Other Craft subjects in which you have a special interest:

. . . .

. . . .

❏ Please send me a free Lark Books Catalog featuring books, kits, and gifts.

Name . . . .

Address . . . .

. . . .

State/Province . . . . Zip/Postal Code . . . .

Lark Books

. . . *Celebrating the Creative Spirit*

Look for Lark Books at your favorite bookstore or crafts supply shop. Distributed by Random House, Inc.